QUESTAR PUBLISHERS, INC.

The GIFT OF SELF-ESTEEM

Give Your Kids a Lasting Treasure

JOE WHITE

QUESTAR PUBLISHERS, INC.
Sisters, Oregon

THE GIFT OF SELF-ESTEEM

Published by Questar Publishers, Inc.

Printed in the United States of America

ISBN 0-945564-09-0

Scripture passages quoted in this book include excerpts from the from the *New American Standard Bible*, © 1960, 1962, 1963, 1971, 1972, 1973, 1975, 1977 by the Lockman Foundation; and *The Holy Bible: New International Version*, © 1973, 1978, 1984 by the International Bible Society, and published by Zondervan Bible Publishers.

For information, write to:
Questar Publishers, Inc.
Post Office Box 1720
Sisters, Oregon 97759

to Mom and Dad
who give "the gift"
so consistently

CONTENTS

The GIFT OF SELF-ESTEEM

Give Your Kids a Lasting Treasure

PART ONE

MAGIC FEATHERS

Elephant Flight

AFTER SPENDING the last twenty years of my life wiping tears from the heartbroken faces of teens in crisis and soothing the brokenness of parents in desperation, I will firmly assert that no American's death has left a greater void in the hope and goodness of America than that of the one great master of animation.

Walt Disney was like a powerful dam holding back the raging water of pornography and cheap, lewd, box-office thrillers. When Disney died, the dam broke and the giant wall of morally degenerate water rushed into every theater and neighborhood video store from Plymouth Rock to the Golden Gate bridge.

Disney had Michelangelo's brush, Edison's steadfastness, Lincoln's courage, and Mother Teresa's sixth sense for loving little children. As Hollywood's ace of spades in a royal flush, Disney's seemingly unbeatable hand came from his talent and determination to appeal wisely and with dignity to basic issues in human hearts.

One particular masterpiece Disney painted was the story of a baby-faced elephant named Dumbo who had floppy ears that brought jeers and ridicule from everyone in his circus environment. Dumbo was a loser in every way. (For many years I felt just like him.) Even his mom was locked and chained from him in ultimate shame.

In one of the most memorable scenes in animated movie history, Dumbo and his trusty friend, Timothy the mouse, found themselves in a giant tree in the company of five scorning crows.

Dumbo's innocence and the mouse's devoted friendship won the hilarious crows to the elephant's side, and this unusual gathering of creatures became convinced that *Dumbo the elephant could fly* (and that fame and fortune were only a flight away). Dumbo wasn't at all convinced until, by a stroke of genius, the solution came from the beak of one Captain Crow. With a pluck of a black

365 Ways to Tell Your Child ***"I LOVE YOU"***

1. When your child is participating in an athletic event or musical performance — be there watching.
2. Help your son or daughter learn a new skill: riding a bike, making a cake, fixing a flat tire.
3. Walk together with your child some morning all the way to the school bus stop.

(continued)

plume from the tail of a surprised comrade, Captain Crow and the gang convinced Dumbo that this "magic" feather would take him to the heights of success.

Clutching the feather in the end of his trunk, the pachyderm toddler dove into the air. With ears flapping wildly, his mouse friend hanging on for dear life, and five crows bouncing off of a hundred-foot cliff with laughter, Dumbo flew like an bird...into the lap of luxury and the long-awaited company of his beloved mom.

As every watching kid knows, the feather wasn't magic. Its tiny buoyancy could in no way defy the pull of gravity and enable a thousand-pound baby elephant to fly.

But to Dumbo, the feather gave hope.

And "hope does not disappoint..." (Romans 5:5).

TRIBUTES — AND TRAGEDY

MAGIC FEATHERS always make child's play out of the impossible. From the actual pen of a seventeen-year-old boy I know, enjoy with me now another elephant flight in an age when surveys indicate that adolescents seem to have forgotten how to respect their moms:

> My Mom and I have always had a different relationship than everybody else whom I grew up with. She was always there for me, a great Christian example, and a unique parent.

365 Ways to Tell Your Child *"I LOVE YOU"*

(continued)

4. Leave an "I love you" note in your child's school lunch box.
5. Tonight, read a chapter together in your child's favorite book.
6. Memorize a verse in the Bible together.
7. Share a devotional time with your child tomorrow morning before school.

For six months she left me. It was probably the most tearful and hardest six months of my life. I was only six years old and really didn't understand that what was happening was going to totally change my life. You see, my Mom was involved in an accident and was in a hospital 130 miles away.

At that time I didn't understand what "paralyzed" meant. I also wondered why my Mom could no longer walk, but had to ride around in a chair with wheels on it. It totally mystified me.

However, time went on. Even though my Mom was so far away, she made sure that one of her friends picked me up for church each Sunday morning.

Time moved on. My Dad moved out. He didn't desert us, he just moved out for an indefinite number of years. My Mom's life was wrecked, but she looked to God and held her head up high. She cried only when she thought my sister, two brothers, and I were asleep.

Later, as we all grew up, I started playing football. My Mom got up every weekday morning and had me at school by 6:45. (If you have never been around a handicapped person, you don't realize what a big task getting out of bed can be.) I didn't really realize or appreciate just what all she was sacrificing for me.

Now I'm seventeen, a senior in high school, and preparing for my final year at home before I leave for college. I'm finally understanding how wonderful Mom is. She gave me two of the most remarkable gifts she could. First of all she gave me Jesus. She is the most remarkable Christian I know. She gets all her strength from God and above all she knows that He will protect her. I remember times when she would decide to drive across the state to visit relatives, and off she'd go by herself. I've known her to sleep in the car or in a hotel parking lot. When asked why, she has a very simple answer: "It takes too much energy to get out of the car and get into a room — and besides, God takes care of me."

The second gift she gave me was the power to never say "I can't!" Even though she was paralyzed, heartbroken, and often without money, she never said "I can't," even though the odds against her were amazing. Through God, or by her will, or both, she gave her children everything we needed and still had plenty left. Even though I didn't understand what she was doing at times, and didn't even care (that was at the stupidest part of my life), she was always there with what I needed.

The crows gave Dumbo a magic feather to fly like crows. My Mom gave me two magic feathers so I might fly like an eagle.

365 Ways to Tell Your Child ***"I LOVE YOU"***

(continued)

8. When the school bus brings home your child, be there at the curb with a welcome-home smile.
9. Talk together about your favorite memories growing up.
10. Find a new way to *trust* your child by granting a new area of responsibility that he or she would both enjoy and benefit from.

To another high school senior, a magic feather became a quill that wrote this invaluable letter of tribute:

> It was a black Saturday in April and my high school baseball career had just come to an abrupt and painful end. All of my lifelong dreams of playing in the state tournament and being recognized as the best team in the state had just been crushed. We had lost not just to anybody, but to our arch-rivals fifteen miles to the west, whom we had beaten three times earlier that year.
>
> Needless to say, I felt awful. A numb feeling came over me as I looked at all the blank faces of the other seniors.
>
> I just walked down to the bullpen and sat down alone. I felt like the world had just ended. I sat down there and cried for what seemed forever (probably about ten minutes). Then I felt a tap on my shoulder and looked up into the tear-filled eyes of my Dad. He held out his arms and said he'd never been more proud of me. He told me that he loved me, and I could tell he was hurting as badly as I.
>
> I'll never forget that moment. He had done so many things to show how much he loved me before, but that moment when I had hit rock bottom, he was there with me.

365 Ways to Tell Your Child ***"I LOVE YOU"***

(continued)

11. Have a family picnic next Sunday afternoon.
12. Sit in church together.
13. When your child is being punished — undergo the punishment with him (occasionally).
14. After your teenage son or daughter comes in from a date, have popcorn together by the fireplace.

365 Ways to Tell Your Child **"I LOVE YOU"**

(continued)

15. Go out in the snow together and throw snowballs at a target (even a few at each other).
16. This weekend, wait up until your son or daughter comes home (no matter how late).
17. Giving your child a back rub.
18. Walk in the rain and jump puddles together.

To another young heart, the pluck of a magic feather from a parental bouquet precipitated this eternal memory:

> When I was in fourth grade, there was a track meet held by the school faculty for all of the kids. I was to run the 200-meter relay. The time came for us to begin. I was running the last leg of the race. We were ahead and my parents were watching. All of a sudden my foot hit a rock and I went flying. My hands went down and were slashed by the sharp rocks, but I didn't feel them for I was so embarrassed for blowing it for our team. The tears just came to my eyes. Then I saw my Dad running towards me. He came over and picked me up and carried me off the field and soothed my pains. He relieved me of all the built-up pressure. I will remember that as long as I live.

Support. Encouragement. Appreciation.

Magic feathers.

What single factor has been determined to best motivate employees to perform to their full potential? Higher pay? No. Greater benefits? No, again. Shorter hours? No, no. It's the boss who makes them feel good about themselves. *Magic feathers.*

It is reported that in small towns, ninety percent of all

365 Ways to Tell Your Child "I LOVE YOU"

(continued)

19. For a time of reflection together, ask your child: "When you pray, how do you think of God?"
20. *Listen* to your child — with all your attention.
21. If your child goes on an overnight trip, leave an "I love you" note in his or her bag.
22. Sit down together and watch your child's favorite TV show.

shoppers choose their favorite clothing store on the basis of where they feel appreciated. *Magic feathers.*

Every suicidal teen, every teen in abortion's trap, every young drug addict — all have one thing in common, one similar cell in the embryo of their spiraling plight: Low self-esteem. *Someone forgot the magic feathers.*

Lest your children join in the tragic decline...absorb these pages, and learn to give what you can and must.

HEY, YOU'RE SPECIAL

STRONG TRADE BALANCES reduce a nation's debt. Good products make a strong trade balance. Happy workers manufacture good products.

But studies show that six out of ten working Americans don't like their jobs. Most refer to their treatment from "the boss" as the problem.

This country's labor and professional scene is wallpapered with blue- and white-collared shirts whose backs are just waiting to be patted...often! What Beethoven gave to the piano, a good boss must give to the employee (and a good parent to the child): "Hey, pal — you're special!"

Sam Walton of the Walmart chain of department stores gives it personally — and daily — to his truck drivers and sales clerks. His army of employees are crazy about him. But in most companies, that isn't the case.

However urgently the plea for more appreciation sounds from the workplace, an even stronger warning signal is coming from our kids. America's teens don't feel special. I've never counseled one teenage drug addict or sex object or near-suicide victim who really liked himself.

Here's a sampling from my recent mail:

> I am drinking, using drugs, and am mixed up in the sex scene. My parents are going through a five-year divorce. To say I am rebelling is an understatement. I think often of suicide because, to me, life is just a waste of time. My Dad will not have anything to do with me. He has never really gotten to know me and what I stand for. I have the feeling that if he would take the time, he'd be very proud of me. I wish he could see me doing something good and proclaim that I am his little girl.

Take a girl with a self-image like that, stir in an encounter with someone like the 17-year-old boy who wrote the following letter (it was sent to me by accident last summer), and guess what will happen?

> Hey, sweetie, you were soooo incredibly hot. You're everything a man could want. You're beautiful and your body is so fine. I can't wait

365 Ways to Tell Your Child ***"I LOVE YOU"***

(continued)

23. Snuggle in bed together as you tell a good-night story.
24. Have a water-pistol fight (let your kids drench you).
25. When your child expresses a fear — try to remember in your own childhood when you had that same fear, and talk together about it.
26. Skim rocks together on a lake or pond or river.

till you get back home. We're going to spend some awesome time together."

Another teenager's letter gives us the inevitable answer:

I have been dating this guy for a little over two months. I fell for him the first time I ever saw him. There was some sort of adventure about him. I'm sixteen years old and think I'm in love. My mother works from 11 P.M. to 7 A.M. and Daddy is gone a lot. Jason came over the other night and stayed until 4 that morning. No one in my family knows. Anyway, we had sex right here in my house. We talked about it afterwards. He felt it was right and that we should have done it. I didn't and now I think I'm pregnant. The only other person who knows is my best friend. I'm writing to ask what I should do. I can't tell my mother or father. I've always been the one to "bring joy to the family."

Poor self-esteem is at the root of the entire gamut of teenage problems:

Dear Joe,

I am a heavyset teenager, not really extremely overweight, but I am not happy with the way I

365 Ways to Tell Your Child ***"I LOVE YOU"***

(continued)

27. For your eyes only, write down on a slip of paper any unloving attitude you may have felt recently toward your child — perhaps irritation or anger that came too easily about something… or a slowness to offer heartfelt forgiveness for some failure… or a lingering focus on something you perceive as negative in your child's behavior or person-

365 Ways to Tell Your Child **I LOVE YOU**

(continued)

ality. Then shred or burn that slip of paper, offer your feelings to God in a prayer of confession, ask for His perspective, and commit yourself to *living* and *thinking* a stronger love, by God's grace and power.

28. Reminisce about your child's toddler days — and say what a wonderful baby he or she was.

look. People have told me that if I'd only lose about twenty or thirty pounds, I'd be perfect. Every time I get caught doing something wrong, I feel worthless at home and at school. I am very embarrassed when I get in trouble. My father preaches to me that I have to be perfect to go to heaven.

I got tired of being fat so I started fasting for a few days and began to restrict a lot of foods. Then later on I got hungry and would eat more than I should. Then I heard how people ate and made themselves throw up. I thought I could quit when I reached a weight I was happy with, but little did I know that I would never be satisfied with being a normal weight. I went from 160 to 115 in a short amount of time. People would comment on how good I looked for a while, and then they got worried. The weight continued to drop. I was a yellowish-gray color and my bones stuck out. I was sickly proud of my bony appearance. I had finally reached my goal. I was thin, but never thin enough. Every time I tried to stop vomiting and start eating normally, I would gain a pound or two and would immediately go back to starving my body and would lose more weight.

I denied I had a problem even though deep down I needed help desperately. My relationship with guys was very confusing. I loved the attention they gave me now that I was thin. I let them use me and would often go too far with them. I wanted so badly to feel wanted by someone, and they made me feel so secure.

'I Should've Realized...'

WHEN ENCOURAGEMENT doesn't happen at home, it happens wherever there's an opportunity:

Dear Joe:

Hello, my name is Cindy and I'm almost 18. Lately I feel guilty calling myself a Christian. It all started when I met my boyfriend last summer. We're still going out and we're involved with sex and I love him very much and he also loves me. I asked God to forgive me and to lead me back to the right path, but I don't want to leave Mike. Now I'm almost four months pregnant and my parents don't know yet. I'm so scared to tell them, especially my Mom. It'll just kill her. Mike gives me the kind of love that I've never received from anyone else. He makes me feel so special...so important...you know what I mean? Will God forgive me for this?

365 Ways to Tell Your Child "I LOVE YOU"

(continued)

29. On the first cold day of autumn, make and drink hot chocolate together.
30. Have milk and cookies together after school.
31. Say, "I'm proud of you."
32. *Twice* this week, prepare your child's favorite dinner menu.

365 Ways to Tell Your Child *"I LOVE YOU"*

(continued)

33. The next time you take a child to an athletic practice, stay and watch from a distance.
34. Help your child make his bed (occasionally).
35. Help your child clean his room (occasionally).
36. Let your son or daughter select where you eat out (even if it's McDonald's again).

Knowing that most of these kids end up in an abortion clinic, I pleaded with this scared little girl to talk to her mother. Lo and behold, she did! A few weeks later I got this reply. Her dear mother had captured the heart of what this book is about:

> Hello, it's me again. I don't know what I was thinking when I thought I couldn't tell my parents. They are the most wonderful people in the world. I should have realized how much they loved me, and in no way would they ever leave me. My Mom reassures me that she loves me just the same and nothing could ever change that. She even says I'm still perfect in her eyes. Can you believe it!
>
> This experience has caused me to wake up and realize how much I was taking my parents' love for granted. It has also brought my family closer together. I just start to cry every time I think about how wonderful my family is, not to mention the wonderful love and forgiveness God has for me.
>
> This is going to be a very difficult time, being a mother at age 19, but we'll just have to keep praying and take one day at a time. The baby's father and I plan on getting married in the future, and I'm so glad he's by my side too.
>
> Thanks for listening.

365 Ways to Tell Your Child "I LOVE YOU"

(continued)

37. Allow (but don't force) your child to share in the cost of some major item the whole family wants. Let him also be a part of the decision-making process — helping select the color, brand, features, etc.
38. Catch fireflies together and make a living lantern.
39. Go rowing or canoeing together.

SEIZE THE OPPORTUNITY

THE FOURTH-GRADE CLASS squirmed and squealed as a mouse was heard somewhere in the room. The teacher, Mrs. Bereduli, called the class to order, then looked squarely at a pupil named Stevie Morris, who was completely blind.

"Stevie, can you tell us where the mouse is?" Loving and perceptive, Mrs. Bereduli knew this nine-year-old's blindness had left him with a keen sense of hearing — as well as a search for significance.

The class became completely silent. Little Stevie tilted his head slightly to the right. "It's in the trash can. It's a mouse and it's in the trash can by your desk." He was exactly right.

In the months to come, in this boy's frequent moments of discouragement, Mrs. Bereduli would again and again bring up the incident with the mouse in the trash can to remind Stevie of his special listening ability.

His ego changed. So did his name. He grew up to become Stevie Wonder, whose super hearing — plus the encouragement of one special lady — turned a dreaded abnormality into a string of gold records.

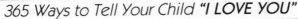

A Pearl, a Rose, a Vision

EVERY RAY OF SUNSHINE, every cloud, every drop of rain in the inward and outward climate of a child's complex everyday life contains a hidden opportunity for encouragement. It may be buried, like a pearl in the obscurity of an oyster shell, patiently awaiting discovery.

Our first child was born to tip the scales in compliancy, meekness, and gentle submission. Jamie is a dream. As soon as I naively patted myself on the back to take the credit, along came number two. Courtney screamed her way into our lives, with a curl on her forehead and a pair of lungs to match the myth. We beat a path to the Christian bookstores and inhaled Dr. Dobson's wonderful advice.

In time the single curl turned into beautiful, long-flowing blond hair. The scream became a personality that would put talent scouts on her doorstep. She's spontaneous, impulsive, emotional, and spins the world on her finger. I can't believe how much I love her. Encouraging that precious middle child has become a favorite pastime.

Last spring we watched what simple encouragement could do: A girl who earlier would completely forget her gymnastics performances and flee to the bench in tears, became a ten-year-old state champion with Olympic potential.

365 Ways to Tell Your Child **"I LOVE YOU"**

(continued)

40. Tell your child about the things you appreciated most about your own parents.
41. Ask your child, "What is your favorite passage in the Bible, and why is it your favorite?"
42. Build a small animal or insect cage together. Then go hunt together for something to put in it.

Last week after school Courtney brought us another oyster. Though buried deeply in an ocean of emotion, I knew the pearl would somehow be found.

"Dad," she said, "guess what?" Her bouncy little eyes were full of something.

"What is it, Courtney?" I knew what was coming.

"Two boys asked me to go with them today." Her big dimples looked like the Grand Canyon.

"Go where?" I joked, in a dad's first nervous experience with the inevitable.

"Oh, Dad, you know. Go with them!"

In sixth grade no less, I thought to myself.

It's true: Being a daddy is not for sissies! I imagine every boy in school will be on our doorstep sometime in the next few years. I'm not sure whether to let any of 'em in. I *am* sure I'm not ready for Courtney to "go with" any guy at this stage.

The next day after Courtney's announcement, a three-page "request" was on our bed. She had listed pros and cons to influence my decision about her admirers. She also listed all the qualities she wanted in a guy, and how one of the boys chasing her just happened to measure up perfectly to each of those qualities (I'm sure!). Courtney wanted to attend a show with him the following night.

Her request left me grasping for an explanation that would say NO, and yet keep Courtney completely on our family team.

365 Ways to Tell Your Child ***"I LOVE YOU"***

(continued)

43. The Bible's love chapter says that "love is patient..." (1 Corinthians 13:4). Have you recently failed to be patient in some way with your child? If so, confess that failure to God, and ask for (and expect) His help in overcoming impatience. Obey His Spirit's prompting whenever He reminds you not to be so up-tight and demanding.

365 Ways to Tell Your Child *"I LOVE YOU"*

(continued)

44. Have a family worship time after a meal — sing together, pray together, read Scripture together.
45. Make up and tell stories with your kids as the heroes.
46. Write a crazy poem together — take turns writing the next line (make sure it rhymes!).
47. Bring home your child's favorite candy bar.

I called the florist and had a red rose delivered to her at school. (I could picture her dimpled blush when the florist made the delivery.) The accompanying note read:

> I can't wait to talk tonight.
> I'll "go with" you forever.
>
> Your #1 boyfriend,
> Daddy

That night the summit began nervously. The beautiful rose was in front of us. I lifted it from the vase.

"Courtney," I said to this bright-eyed sixth-grader, "your life — your body, your heart — is like a beautiful rosebud. Given God's nourishment and His timing, it will bloom one day. Yours will be extremely beautiful. One day you'll put on a pure white wedding gown and you'll begin a walk into the arms of the man of your dreams, a walk of lovely grace that will go on with him for seventy-five years. On that wedding day, Courtney, your rose will be in full bloom."

She looked at me intently, as if putting up with the "fluff" while waiting for the answer.

By this time I had begun pulling the petals off the rose, one at a time. I went on, slowly and deliberately spoiling the flower's beauty.

"Unfortunately, Baby, for many girls there won't be a

365 Ways to Tell Your Child *"I LOVE YOU"*

(continued)

48. Make up and sing songs to your kids about how much you love them.
49. Dream together about a round-the-world, as-long-as-you-like, all-expenses-paid vacation. Talk about the favorite places you would each like to see, and what you would do in each one.

beautiful bloom, because beginning in junior high, boys come along and pull off the petals one at a time. Each guy takes his petal, then moves on. The outside petals are innocent little "go steady" petals. Then there's holding hands, then a kiss, then a long kiss that leads to petting and that leads to intercourse, and that leads to regret."

Now the flower was stripped and ugly.

"Courtney, you are a priceless flower, the finest in the world. Your husband deserves the whole rose. For the beauty of your wedding day, your Mom and I are saying no to steady boyfriends for a few years until your maturity is in bloom."

At first there were tears. The next day we were teammates.

Pearl discovered. Daddy relieved. Little girl with a vision.

Here's a letter I just received from a girl who never received the vision:

> It is just so incredibly hard for me to say "no" to a guy. I mean, sometimes I could just sit down and cry for hours because of the person I have become. If anyone knew how many guys I had slept with, I would be considered a slut! And that word hits me so hard! When I hear people say, "Oh she's a slut!" I think, if they only knew about me, they could say that to me.

Joe, I don't want to have to feel like I owe anything to any of the guys I go out with, especially not my body. I need someone to help me. I can't do it by myself. The reason I'm telling you all of this is because I know that you do care about me even though I can be a brat! I'm really sorry for that. Almost all of my friends have had sex before and I didn't know that until after I had. Of course, that's not the main subject most girls talk about. But it is what a lot of guys talk about and all they want from certain girls. I mean, I could have used some of those guys as easy as they used me. Because you were right in your talk the other day about sex. It is fun! And that's a main excuse, I guess. But it is very wrong. I know and I don't want to have to feel like I have or want to do it any more.

I know that I'm very lucky that I'm not pregnant. I have so much guilt inside me. And I really think it's time for me to stop and just say "no." When a guy wants anything because they can't love me now, or wants to have sex for that reason, they're too young.

I don't know what to do, could you please try to help me?"

We can't begin too soon to give our kids the base of self-esteem they need to make the right choices.

365 Ways to Tell Your Child **"I LOVE YOU"**

(continued)

50. Take an evening walk together.
51. Make a telephone call to your child, just to say you're thinking of him.
52. Have a pillow fight together some night at bedtime.
53. Play games together — Old Maid, Concentration, Candyland, Sorry, Pictionary.

There's probably an oyster waiting in your home right now.

Ready to go pearl diving?

ON THE SPOT

MY SWEET WIFE gave me four wonderful children, but pregnancy and childbirth didn't go easy with her. I was so grateful for #1 child — yet even more grateful for #4 child's Mom.

We began our family in a one-bedroom house. Debbie Jo's response to my appetite for lots of kids was the motto, "One more kid, one more room." So we built rooms.

By the time our fourth child arrived, our house had taken a beating, and it was time for remodeling. As we knocked out the south wall, Debbie Jo had a choice: Either build a dining room over the playroom, or have no dining room and let the playroom have an eighteen-foot ceiling. She decided in favor of her kids.

Boy, was I excited. I found a sale and bought a trampoline for fifty dollars, and it now sits wall-to-wall in the playroom. In the evenings, the kids and I fairly live on it.

Besides being great fun, trampolines offer good object lessons on success-building. For example, when a kid is learning new tricks, someone else — a "spotter" — needs to be standing beside the trampoline, alertly watching and ready to lend a guarding hand if a wrong move sends the

365 Ways to Tell Your Child ***"I LOVE YOU"***

(continued)

54. Rake leaves together — then jump in them.
55. Have a family water balloon fight (with *you* as the prime target).
56. The Bible's love chapter says that "love is kind…" (1 Corinthians 13:4). Think of a special way you can show *kindness* to your child today.

*365 Ways to Tell Your Child **"I LOVE YOU"***

(continued)

57. Go apple or berry picking together, then take some to neighbors.
58. At the beach or in a park sandbox, play tic-tac-toe in the sand.
59. Make cookies together; then put them on neighbors' porches, ring the doorbell, and run.

jumper too close to the edge. The spotter is ready to jump in if there is a major problem. A good spotter is also a motivator, encouraging and complimenting the jumper.

This kind of "spotting" is what our kids need in life — though, as you think about this subject, some good questions arise:

Can parents be overprotective?

Don't some parents baby their kids too much?

Do kids need their distance?

Do kids need to fail a little at times?

Shouldn't parents back off a little when kids get older?

Yes, to all the above. Dad shouldn't be on the sidelines screaming at the refs, at the coach, and at his kid. Mom shouldn't be hiding her fourteen-year-old behind her apron anymore.

But good parents are good spotters. They're always close enough to encourage, to give credit, to provide guidance, to step in if major failure is looming.

The secret is balance. Soft parents are usually way too soft. Harsh parents are usually way too harsh. (Sound like the Three Bears?) Good spotters — with the right balance — are a rare breed.

I never collected baseball cards, but Brady likes them. So I "spot" him by learning enough about them to help him become a good collector.

365 Ways to Tell Your Child "I LOVE YOU"

(continued)

60. Make homemade ice cream together.
61. Talk together about your favorite characters in the Bible. Why do you admire them? In what ways do you identify with them?
62. Ask your child: "If you could live inside an animal for a day, what animal would you choose?"

I can barely do a headstand, but Courtney loves gymnastics. So we "spot" her by stuffing fifty-dollar trampolines and homemade balance beams into Santa's bag, and also by sitting in the stands at every gymnastics meet.

I work hard to develop friendships with boys who pay attention to my daughters. With all the kids running around us, Debbie Jo and I could sometimes be accused of not having friends our own age — but a good spotter has to stay on the edge of the action!

If you'd like to spend an invaluable two hours some evening, sit down with your spouse (or, if you're a single parent, do it alone with God), and prepare a simple "spotting" plan.

First, take a sheet of paper and divide it into three side-by-side columns. In the left column, list your child's activities. In the middle column, list possible "spotting" actions you as a parent could take to encourage and truly help your child in this activity. In the right column, list any thoughts about "spotting distance": In what ways might you get too "close" to allow your child to feel successful? In what ways might you be tempted to be too "far," and possibly allow too much failure or mediocrity?

Your home probably doesn't have a room designed for trampolines… but I promise you, your family has a child designed for spotting.

THE ONE-MINUTE PARENT?

I HAVE A GOOD FRIEND whose great success as the owner of a large TV station has been surpassed only by his great success as a father. He has some of the neatest kids I know. Recently he asked me what I thought of the idea that parents should concentrate on spending "quality time" with their kids.

I said, "I think it's important."

To my surprise he replied, "I think it's baloney! I believe in *Q U A N T I T Y* time!" He drew the word out to help me feel his meaning. "I believe you've got to chip away at it every day," he continued. "Kids need our time, and lots of it — regularly."

We're good at making up pet slogans — such as "quality time, not quantity" — that are only cop-outs, yet we convince ourselves we've developed a sound new concept in parenting. I believe this "one-minute manager, one-minute parent" syndrome has really got some parents fooled. Kids are not one-minute people. They are twenty-four-hour-a-day people with twenty-four-hour-a-day appetites for encouragement.

Today has been one of my most crunching days. But a short while ago the phone rang, and my eighth-grade daughter told me she had a thirty-minute wait at school between the end of her classes and a trip for a volleyball

365 Ways to Tell Your Child **"I LOVE YOU"**

(continued)

63. Plant trees in your yard in honor of your kids (one for each kid).
64. Take nature hikes together — collect leaves, acorns, rocks, moss, sticks, and whatever.
65. On a hot day, hook up a water hose and sprinkler in the back yard, and run through the water together.

game. I made a quick run by McDonald's and picked up a hamburger and met her at school to fill that thirty-minute window.

Oh, how those times are fleeting!

Last week I was scheduled to be interviewed by telephone on the subject of parenting. The recorded interview was to be broadcast by radio on a program heard by about a quarter of a million people. Unfortunately, after making the commitment to the interview we discovered it was coming at the same time as one of my daughter's volleyball games. I fought a raging inner battle: I couldn't walk out on the interview, but I knew that to my little girl the stands at the gym would seem empty without her Daddy there watching.

When the program host called just before the scheduled interview, I pleaded my case. With trembling voice I began, "Dan, I want you to know I'm happy to do this, and we've committed to doing it. But a few minutes from now my little girl will be serving the volleyball in a critical game. Is there any way we can reschedule the interview?" His response was one-hundred-percent positive: "I'm a single parent of four, and I appreciate so much your decision to put your kids ahead of the media. Go ahead," he said enthusiastically, "and we'll do the interview later." I jumped in the car and flew to the game.

Nothing in family life gives more sheer enjoyment than the opportunity of watching your kids in a success experience. In playing on the eighth-grade volleyball team, my

365 Ways to Tell Your Child ***"I LOVE YOU"***

(continued)

66. Give everyone a dollar (or some other prudent amount) and go shopping together just for the fun of it.
67. As a family, have a make-your-own peanut-butter-specialty-sandwich party. To start, spread peanut butter on bread; as toppings, use apple and banana slices, chocolate chips, marshmallows, and raisins.

365 Ways to Tell Your Child *"I LOVE YOU"*

(continued)

68. Roast marshmallows together in the fireplace.
69. Make candy-covered apples together.
70. Shop together for a model plane or ship, then build it together.
71. The Bible's love chapter says that love "is not proud…" (1 Corinthians 13:4). If some unwanted "distance" has recently

daughter Jamie had struggled with her serve and almost everything else. But several evenings of practice together had brought noticeable improvement.

When I walked into the gym, the stands were roaring with nervous excitement. Our team was behind 15 to 14 — and Jamie was at the serving line. I broke out in a cold sweat.

She served the first ball like a rifle shot. A girl on the other side got her hand on it just before it went out of bounds. 15-15!

Jamie looked across the net, and seemed as steady as the Prudential rock. My stomach was an earthquake.

She tossed up the ball, and again smashed it over the net and off the arm of a surprised opponent. 16-15! One more point would win the game. I'm sure an EKG test on me at that moment would have put me in a class with heart-attack victims.

Jamie's third serve was another ace — the most beautiful I've ever seen. Everybody went crazy, and my little girl's teammates swarmed around her like world-series champions dogpiling the winning pitcher after the seventh game.

It was the greatest moment in sports history for me. What if I hadn't been there? Opportunities in business come and go like freight trains…but those special times with our children are more precious than diamonds.

365 Ways to Tell Your Child *"I LOVE YOU"*

(continued)

come between you and your child, ask yourself if any pride on your part is hindering a quick return to closeness.

72. Spend a special time praying together for others: for your leaders and teachers in your church, for government leaders, for any missionaries your child knows, for neighbors, for friends, for family members.

ENCORE!

LAST SUMMER AT OUR CAMP, a teenage girl — a talented musician — told me this memorable story:

"My voice teacher had scheduled a recital at which all the students would perform for their parents. I was to sing an Italian piece I'd been working hard at learning."

"As usual, I absent-mindedly forgot to tell Daddy until the night before the recital. He had been traveling a lot because of a big oil and gas deal he was working on, and told me he was to leave on a trip the next day and wouldn't be able to attend the recital. My heart dropped. I dreaded having to stand up and perform without Daddy there smiling at me.

"But the show must go on, as they say, and it did. The next night I walked on stage without feeling any excitement, and nodded to my teacher to start the piece. Then, as I lifted my head, my eyes met with my father's — and I'm sure I've never sung that Italian piece better."

BREAKFAST ON THE BAYOU

ONE OF MY FAVORITE teenage friends, a boy from Louisiana, let me know that guys need encouragement as much as girls do — and the smallest little incidents can mean the very most. His story is worth repeating:

"I had been fishing on the bayou most of the morning. It was hot, I hadn't caught much, and I was hungry. Half-heartedly I kept on.

"Soon I heard a noise from the woods on the bank in front of me. As the noise came closer, I began to make out a little short, black-haired lady picking her way through the woods. She called out my name — and I was a little embarrassed as the other fishermen around me gave me funny looks. But I quickly lost that feeling and became very proud — because I was the only guy out there whose mom brought him breakfast. She took time to find me and spend time with me when I needed it most."

That wise mom is leaving a legacy loaded with smiles.

TOMAHAWK TOM

TOM HUND is a Kansas farm boy who rekindles your dreams of the wonderful down-home folk who labor tirelessly in America's breadbasket to feed our hungry nation and much of the world. Dominating Tom's lean, six-foot-ten frame is a mile-wide smile spreading across his All-American face.

In his college days, "Tomahawk Tom" spent two summers on our camp counseling staff. That was years ago, but the memory of his contagious countenance still looms around the camp. Tom had a healthy self-image that I would wish — oh, how I would wish! — for every American kid. His stable Christian faith and his commit-

*365 Ways to Tell Your Child **"I LOVE YOU"***

(continued)

73. Imagine together that you had a time machine, and could go back to any era in history. What time period would you most want to visit?
74. Make a tree house together.
75. Say (with a big hug), "You're my favorite son." When he says, "But I'm you only son," answer, "But you're still my favorite."

ment to loving children were like a banner flying high above a ship on a voyage of continual discovery. I watched him constantly bouncing across camp, patting people on the back and breathing out words of encouragement as regularly as his own air. Tom has the gift.

To everyone he meets, Tom Hund is just plain delicious.

And Tom Hund has 16 brothers and 6 sisters.

Yep — a total of twenty-three kids in one family...and at one time during Tom's teenage years, twenty of them were living together in the same small Kansas farmhouse. Mr. and Mrs. Hund stacked 'em in like sardines — four to a bed, twenty toes facing east and twenty facing west.

Twenty-three kids! Imagine calling them by name to supper! Or keeping track of their birthdays (and planning a party each time)!

In God's sovereign and mysterious quilting process, two tragedies were woven together to bring together at the altar a single mom of twelve and a single father of eleven. It was the making of one of the most interesting families ever assembled (or squeezed) under one roof.

I met together with Tom and his parents because I had to know how two people — parents just like you and me, except that they had so much more parenting to do — could be able in such demanding circumstances to build the good stuff so securely into their kids, as evidenced to me by the life of their long and lanky son Tom. Tom remembered it like this:

*365 Ways to Tell Your Child **"I LOVE YOU"***

(continued)

76. The night your child says he's running away from home, fix his favorite dinner.
77. Listen appreciatively as your child practices his first trumpet lesson.
78. When you sense something is troubling your child, make a reason for a trip in the car alone with him.

365 Ways to Tell Your Child **"I LOVE YOU"**

(continued)

79. Plan and carry out a treasure hunt — at home, in the back yard, in the neighborhood, at the park, or all of them combined.
80. Press your child's band uniform before each performance.
81. Go to court with your child when he pays his first speeding ticket.

"Mom and Dad were always there for us...always. We're a family-centered family. We ate every meal together, worked together, played together, fought together, and made up together. Dad had an old blue bus that we'd load up to travel together and go to church together."

(Sounds like that *together* word might be a clue to their success, huh?)

"Mom and Dad devoted themselves to us. Dad did our daily farm chores with us. We had long talks about right and wrong while milking cows, and interesting father-son discussions while we cleaned the stalls and fed the hogs. While the seventeen boys did the outside work with Dad, the six girls did the cooking and inside work with Mom. (We ate lots of potatoes!)

"Dad was quiet and soft-spoken. I think his example as a good man spoke most loudly to us. He treated Mom really well. Because he respected her, we did too (except for maybe a few times when we'd get playful and put a fake rubber black snake beside her on the porch...but she was a great sport about things like that.) Dad found time for small-group talks with us, and somehow got around to each of us regularly for one-on-one time. That's when our character sunk in. Dad's way of encouragement was a genuine pat on the back and something nice to say. I knew he cared."

When Tom told me he didn't remember many spankings, his dad smiled and held up the hickory stick as if used only yesterday.

82. Have fun together answering this: What would be the most exciting surprise that could happen to you tomorrow?
83. Pretend you're a team of television writers asked to develop a new TV adventure series. What would be the setting for the series, what would the major characters be like, and what would you name them?

"From the time we were babies we were taught right and wrong," Tom continued. "We did what was expected or we were in trouble. Discipline was more of a lifestyle in our house. Mom and Dad were loving but also strict and stuck by their word. We learned that we didn't always get our own way. They taught us to be unselfish.

"Mom was an encourager. I always knew she believed in me. Somehow she'd make it to my basketball games and she'd always tell me how well I played. Although Mom had to work many hours each week as a nurse to make ends meet, she devoted the rest of her time entirely to her husband and kids.

"Our family wasn't perfect. We had our fights. It was a real challenge for these two giant families to blend together into one, but Mom and Dad had consistency and commitment. That's what made it work. And when I accepted Christ into my heart in high school, He truly brought it all together for me."

Tom's father spoke up, with words that were few but wise: "My Dad taught me to mean what you say, and to find the good qualities in each child."

He continued: "We didn't have money to sidetrack us. Too much money is not good for kids. On the farm everyone worked together. We lived day by day, and the good Lord took care of us."

With a chuckle, Mrs. Hund added, "I'm glad it's over…but all in all it was fun." She also talked about her method of encouragement: "I tried to spread my love around. I always liked to listen to each one. I hugged and kissed them often. At night I'd make the rounds and ask each one how his or her day was, and we'd say prayers together."

I told her she was a great mom. She blushed and said, "I hope so. Some day I'll know for sure."

For those of us who happen to have fewer than twenty-three children, I hope the Hunds' story has warmed your heart, and strengthened your resolve to never let the "I'm too busy" line keep you from spending time together with your kids.

PROFILES IN ENCOURAGEMENT

A LOVING MOM spent hundreds of hours walking through the woods with her daughter — her eyes full of wonder. They felt the leaves, touched the moss to her tiny face, observed the smallest creatures. Young Rachel Carson grew up to awaken us to the fragile vulnerability of our environment in her book *Silent Spring.*

A twenty-year-old woman reached her arms around a "hopeless" child — a blind, deaf, speechless girl who screamed like a wildcat in fits of rage, violently thrashing her surroundings. As patience and encouragement transcended time, Annie Sullivan filled Helen Keller with hope — and history books glow with tributes to them both.

365 Ways to Tell Your Child "I LOVE YOU"

(continued)

84. Stay up to talk together after your son or daughter's first date.
85. Keep a scrapbook of your child's awards, newspaper clippings, photos, etc. Get it out often and look at it together.
86. If your child is participating in the Christmas parade, be there on the cold street to watch him.

He was a skinny, backwoods boy whose family's humble means could afford for his education little more than a fireplace to read by. But he became so inspired by the encouragement of his mom that he said years later, "All that I ever became I owe to my angel mother." What he became was President of the United States — Abraham Lincoln.

A poor, black four-year-old with deformed legs and only a slight chance to walk had a working mom who believed in her — and took her once a week to therapy sessions hundreds of miles away. The sessions involved countless hours of leg massage, a therapy the mother continued tirelessly at home. From the mother's example the girl's brothers and sisters caught the love and understood the sacrifice, and they too joined in to give their sister both massages and hope. This went on for years, and the little girl not only walked — she *ran.* Those deformed legs became the golden pistons of Wilma Rudolph, perhaps the finest female runner who ever lived.

He was a terrified, runaway fisherman. But into his bloodstream the resurrected Christ shot hope, and it sent Peter from the depths of denial and despair to the peak of world impact.

Encouragement. It can take a young girl who enjoys the woods, a raging blind and deaf mute, a gangling country

365 Ways to Tell Your Child ***"I LOVE YOU"***

(continued)

87. Look together at a road atlas, write your initials on each state you've visited, and talk about your memories of these visits.
88. Let your child teach you to roller skate.
89. The Bible's love chapter says that love "is not rude..." (1 Corinthians 13:5). Have you in any way failed to show the right respect and simple courtesy to your child? Ask God to

365 Ways to Tell Your Child "I LOVE YOU"

(continued)

remind you of any failure in this area, and if you've been guilty — confess the sin immediately, and go as soon as possible to ask for forgiveness from your child.

90. Invite your son's or daughter's friends to your home to spend the night.
91. Know when report card day is, and ask to see it.

boy, a crippled daughter and sister, a despondent disciple — and place them in history's hall of fame.

It's happened throughout the ages, and it still happens today.

A church worker gave the right encouragement to a talented fifteen-year-old girl with curly hair and a guitar — and now, with an on-target musical message of love, Amy Grant passes on that encouragement to countless young people (and their parents) around the world.

It was time for another Olympic extravaganza, and *Sports Illustrated* predicted the United States couldn't contend for a medal in an event entered by the graceful American diver Michele Mitchell. But she won the silver medal — and gave this credit to her source of energy: "Before each dive I looked at my Dad for the last-minute 'go-for-it' look he gives me.... For the rest of my life I will always remember that silent language we exchanged.... It's one of those memories that remains etched forever in my mind."

My Mom and Dad have given encouragement to each other throughout fifty-one years of marriage...and still do consistently. They hold hands and kiss and eat dinner by candlelight.

365 Ways to Tell Your Child *"I LOVE YOU"*

(continued)

92. Show genuine concern when your child says he is sick and can't go to school that day. Take his temperature, and ask if you should make an appointment with the doctor.
93. Take a half-hour, silent walk through a park or through the woods together; when the half-hour is over, talk together about what you observed and what you were thinking.

Four gracious little packages that span ages six to fourteen — and who call me "Daddy" — constantly give the gift to me, with grace and dignity. In my line of work, I need it every day.

Encouragement. It builds up young and old, parent and child, husband and wife. It gives direction to a confused teenager, worth to a secretary, hope to a single parent, value to a spouse. It adds zip to anyone's step.

And giving it can be as natural as breathing.

PARDNER

BURDENED BY DEEP DEPRESSION, Jill traveled for two days to the youth retreat on Padre Island, Texas, and joined sixty teenagers for a spring break on the Gulf Coast beach.

While there, she spoke of suicide.

I dropped in on the retreat to speak to the kids. Fortunately the family contingent I brought along included Pardner, my grandmom who was then in her late eighties. With her East Texas country charm, Pardner came alongside this troubled seventeen-year-old as naturally as if Jill were her own.

That was several years ago, but Jill now recalls that life-saving weekend as if it were yesterday. "Pardner and I would take long walks on the beach every morning around sunrise," Jill remembers. "She told me I could make it. She gave me courage to go back and face my problems. I wanted to listen to her because she listened to me. She made me feel I was the most important person on earth. I never had anyone care for me like Pardner did."

Jill is now the top counselor on our summer camp staff of a thousand-plus collegians.

As she showed Jill, Pardner has a gift that she unwraps daily, the gift called encouragement. Pardner is a hope-builder...and "hope does not disappoint." Pardner's magic would fill Houdini with wonder, yet her gift is really a method available to all.

All who visit Pardner learn more about it. They walk out of her house with two new possessions. One is in their hand: perhaps a piece of freshly baked cake, a handful of dimes, a jar of homemade preserves, or a hand-trimmed apron. The other is in their heart: the memory of her "you can do it" smile, and her encouraging words filled with "go-for-it-ness."

Pardner's gift of encouragement came into full-bloom in her days as a young single parent of my Mom. Pardner went the distance alone — and did the job well. Her "little chick" has always had a full cup of healthy self-esteem, because Pardner kept pouring into it. With excellence and grace, Mom also practices this hope-building, continuing a chain reaction that Pardner began. That's the way encouragement works in the life of any kid or spouse or employee: When we fill up their cup, it overflows to others.

365 Ways to Tell Your Child ***"I LOVE YOU"***

(continued)

94. Have fun together answering this question: What famous person living today would you most like to meet and talk with?
95. Build a "Faith Growth Chart" on which you list prayers and answers in one column, and memorized Bible verses in another. See your child's faith grow!

I've watched her potty-train a one-year-old better than Dr. Spock, redirect a rebellious eighteen-year-old like a Barnum & Bailey lion-tamer, care for a community of retired adults like a skilled psychologist — and bring lasting hope into the heart of a suicidal, seventeen-year-old girl. All along Pardner's footsteps, the seeds she has sown have grown into blooming flowers that brighten everyone's life — including her own. (Recently, on her ninety-fifth birthday, a total of 122 unsolicited visitors dropped by her home to give their greetings.)

Five heart attacks haven't slowed down this nearly century-old ray of heavenly light, but a raging battle with shingles and cataracts have begun to weaken her. Yet her smile never dims. Her eyes continue to sparkle. And the gift keeps on giving.

Once *you* have discovered the joy of giving this gift — as a parent, a boss, a spouse, a friend, a child — prepare yourself for a new chapter in your life, a chapter filled with more exclamation points than you ever dreamed were possible.

Heyday Holidays

TODAY IS DECEMBER 26, and do you know what I learned yesterday? It's not how much you spend that counts; it's how you spend it, and how you wrap it.

Hitting four kids on-target with the right presents has always been an interesting challenge for this progressive

365 Ways to Tell Your Child **"I LOVE YOU"**

(continued)

96. After a family picnic in the park, have everyone browse and explore to find something that represents to them some aspect of God. Then come together and take turns telling what you found and what it means to you. (An example: A black-eyed susan illustrates how God wants to be the center of our lives [like the flower's black center]. When we have

365 Ways to Tell Your Child "I LOVE YOU"

(continued)

Him truly at the center, all the parts of our lives form a beautiful and orderly whole — like the arrangement of the flower's petals in a perfect circle.)

97. When you shop for clothing for yourself, take along your child and ask for his opinion on what he thinks looks best on you.

daddy. But in our house, I don't know when Santa Claus ever had more fun than this Christmas.

As I tucked the kids in bed last night, I asked them what their favorite presents were.

Courtney pointed out her first leather Bible with her name printed on the cover. What made this gift number one is that she already owns a lot of the content in that book; it's truly *hers*. She's memorized lots of Scripture, giving her not only spiritual input and guidance but also a great sense of personal accomplishment. (Last year Courtney's favorite gift was a small book she wrote. It's her handiwork, and she doesn't care that only one copy was printed! We had it illustrated and hardbound at a cost of about fifteen dollars. She still proudly displays it on a shelf in front of her favorite dolls.)

Brady's favorite gift was more baseball cards. Why? They're his hobby. His skill and organizational abilities have made that collection a great one.

Jamie's favorite gift was one she gave me — a poem she wrote and had calligraphied and framed, all on her own initiative.

Cooper said his favorite all-time gift was a two-wheel scooter — and a daddy who ran around with him until he could stay up on it.

I believe it's worth the trouble to really go all out and have a heyday on holidays. And this year we worked hard to "wrap it up" in meaning. The kids and I researched the

365 Ways to Tell Your Child "I LOVE YOU"

(continued)

98. Taking cameras for each kid, go on a scavenger hunt to find and take pictures of God's many different creations. Make a scrapbook or poster with the photographs; then show them in an after-dinner presentation for grandparents and friends.
99. Make popcorn, curl up together on the couch, and watch your son or daughter's favorite video.

Scriptures that underlie the songs and symbols of Christmas. Then the *kids* conducted a candlelight service for their parents, grandparents, and great-grandparents.

What's the litmus test for successful gift selection — and for making each holiday a mountain-top experience? *Give your kids opportunities to succeed...and then compliment those successes!*

Creative Christmases

WE LIVE IN A NEIGHBORHOOD full of kid-loving parents, and we wondered how they made each Christmas a peak celebration in their homes. Now that another December 25 is over, we've made the rounds to ask them about it (Monday morning quarterbacks are always the best informed!).

Here's what they told us they did — and they share these ideas as gifts to you and me:

- ☆ When you put up the nativity scene, let each family member choose one or more of the characters — Mary, Joseph, the wise men, etc. Then each of you can look up information about them in the Bible, and tell the others what you find.
- ☆ When Christmas is over, keep Christmas cards in a basket. Read aloud several of them each night at dinner, and pray together for the person or family

who sent each one. Do this until you've gone through all of the cards. (A variation of this idea: In the days and weeks before Christmas, follow this nightly procedure at dinner using the cards that arrived in the mail that day.)

☆ On Christmas Eve, gather around a lighted candle. As you sing *Silent Night*, have each child light his own hand-held candle from the main candle, then continue singing as you walk by candlelight to bed.

☆ No matter what the extended family wants us to do - we always have Christmas morning at our own house.

☆ Make or buy a new ornament for each family member each year, and have everyone put his own ornament on the tree. (Be sure to let each child put his ornament anywhere he wants, and resist the temptation to move it to a "better" spot.) Years from now, when the kids have grown up and gone to homes of their own, they'll already have the beginning of their own ornament collection.

☆ On December 1, draw names among family members, and have secret buddies for the rest of the month until Christmas. Do special things to let your secret buddy know he or she is loved, and that Christ Jesus came because God loved us. Then make the revealing of your secret buddies' names a special part of your Christmas Eve or Christmas Day celebration.

365 Ways to Tell Your Child "I LOVE YOU"

(continued)

100. Have a surprise make-your-own-sundae ice cream party, making sure your child's favorite toppings are all served.
101. As you do household chores, let your child help in everything — even if it takes four times as long to complete them.
102. After a scolding, tell your child, "Did you know I love you even when you're naughty?" Then give him a hug.

☆ If you live in an area where it's possible, cut down your own Christmas tree — and let each child saw or chop a little!

☆ Bake a birthday cake for Jesus and sing "Happy Birthday" to Him on Christmas Day.

☆ Exchange "word" gifts. Draw names among family members, then think of a good word that describes the person whose name you've drawn. Use your creativity to make a gift that incorporates that word — for example, a gift engraved or inscribed with the word plus a verse of Scripture. Present your word gifts to one another on Christmas morning.

☆ Bake Christmas goodies together for friends and neighbors, and go together as a family to deliver them personally.

☆ Make cookie ornaments to hang on the tree, in windows, and throughout your home. Allow each of the kids to eat one or two each day.

☆ Don't forget our feathered friends. Make a family project of decorating a tree outside with birdseed balls, orange baskets, and yards and yards of strung popcorn — and enjoy watching the birds feast. (Remember to continue feeding them throughout the winter; once they've found a source of food, they'll keep coming back!)

☆ Put a cradle under the Christmas tree. Each time your children do something commendable, place a piece of cloth or a cotton ball (or anything soft) into

365 Ways to Tell Your Child ***"I LOVE YOU"***

(continued)

103. The Bible's love chapter says that love "is not easily angered..." (1 Corinthians 13:5). Is it truly *difficult* for you to become angry with your child? Or is it far too easy? For your own benefit as well as your child's, evaluate yourself honestly in this regard.

104. Ask for your child's opinion on a big family decision.

365 Ways to Tell Your Child **"I LOVE YOU"**

(continued)

105. Show him where you've kept for a long time a special card or picture he's given you.
106. Never say "I'm too busy."
107. Pretend together that you were chosen to join a space voyage to another galaxy, a trip that would take several years. What would you take with you?

the cradle. When Jesus is born on Christmas morning, He'll have a soft bed to sleep in.

☆ After coming home from caroling or attending a Christmas Eve service at church, sit by the fire and enjoy peppermint ice cream, Christmas cookies, and each other. This can become one of the best sharing and prayer times together of the year.

☆ Take a family photograph by the tree each year. Make a copy for each child's scrapbook so someday he can share it with his own family.

☆ On Christmas day, go out and *give*. Spend a portion of the day (or the day before) doing something for the needy, such as serving in soup lines, taking food, clothing, or toys to poor families, or singing and visiting with residents of a nursing home.

HOPE-FILLED BIRTHDAYS

I'LL NEVER FORGET my treasure hunt birthday presents. Mom would go to great lengths to polish the money in the treasure chest and run me all over the yard and house from clue to clue, until I finally found the gold!

Here are other ideas that we and our neighbors use to encourage our kids on their most special day.

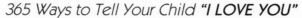

108. For your spouse's birthday or for Mother's Day or Father's Day, be a partner with your child in planning and making (or doing) something special for your spouse. Offer suggestions and assistance as appropriate to help make it a successful creative experience for your child.

- Host a "bring-a-dollar" party. Everyone goes with the birthday child to a local discount store to purchase his favorite gift with the pooled dollars.
- Set your alarm clocks so everyone else gets up before the birthday person does on the morning of his or her birthday. Then converge on the celebrity with wake-up hugs and gifts.
- Plan a scavenger hunt — to find the guests for the party! Have refreshments and games prepared for when everyone is rounded up.
- Let the birthday person choose the menu for dinner, and the fun activities afterward. You could even let the birthday person plan the menu for all three meals that day.
- Have a breakfast birthday party, and let the honoree be free from chores for the day.
- Plan a hayride and cookout.
- Serve breakfast in bed to the birthday person, with the rest of the family serving as waiters.
- Serve dinner with fine china, silver, and candlelight — even if it's only hamburgers — for the birthday person and his special guests.
- Have a costume party.
- Have a come-as-you-are breakfast party — awaken the guests by surprise, and give them only a few minutes to slip into something and meet for breakfast.

- Decorate your home with birthday balloons, posters, and streamers.
- Make the birthday a special Daddy-kid day. Make sure Dad has cleared his calendar so he can spend the entire day making the child feel special — playing together, shopping together...whatever activities the child enjoys.

"Mountaintops" — such as holidays, birthdays, and graduation days — are all great excuses for building the level of hope, happiness, and encouragement in your kids. Life isn't lived on a mountaintop — but the special experiences there can nourish the quality of your child's life in the day-to-day valleys throughout the year.

Most Meaningful

THINGS DON'T SATISFY. Never have...never will.

But *things* are so often what Americans build their lives around. We make up six percent of the world's population, yet we absorb forty percent of the world's resources. We eat seventy-five acres of pizza a day, seventeen million eggs, three million gallons of ice cream, and three thousand tons of candy. We also drive forty-five thousand new cars off the showroom floors. We have plenty of *things*. Yet our kids are the most dissatisfied, hardest-to-please kids the world has ever known, and are

365 Ways to Tell Your Child ***"I LOVE YOU"***

(continued)

109. With every "Good morning" and "Good night," give your child a hug.
110. Give your child your full attention when he tells you what happened at school today, and provide a thoughtful response.

involved in more crime and more illegal drug use than kids in any nation on earth.

Last summer I asked two thousand "professional" teenagers to tell me the most meaningful thing their parents had done for them. Lots of sixteen-year-olds contributed answers — but new cars were surprisingly absent from the list. Many seventeen- and eighteen-year-olds gave us input — but none of them mentioned jewelry or expensive senior trips.

This selected list represents accurately what the kids mentioned most:

- *We begin and end each day with "I love you."*
- *My parents listen to my stories, even when they're boring.*
- *My parents set aside special times just to be with me.*
- *My parents are busy, but never too busy for me.*
- *They tell me I am someone special.*
- *My parents tell me they are proud of me!*
- *Though my parents aren't strong Christians, they encourage me in my own walk with God.*
- *They give me responsibility, showing they trust me.*
- *They don't say, "I told you so" even when I make mistakes.*
- *My dad started eating breakfast with me.*

365 Ways to Tell Your Child **"I LOVE YOU"**

(continued)

111. Volunteer to be a homeroom mom or dad on a special day at school.
112. Make pancakes shaped like animals, footballs, flowers, your child's initials, etc.
113. Buy a box of paper clips, and have a timed contest to see who can make the longest chain in one minute. (If you need

365 Ways to Tell Your Child *"I LOVE YOU"*

(continued)

to handicap yourself to make the contest a fair one, put your pile of paper clips in the next room, and allow yourself to get only one at a time to bring back and add to your chain.)

114. Have fun together answering this question: If you could go back in time, what famous person in history would you most like to meet and talk with?

- *My Mom stays up late with me so I can talk about my problems.*
- *My parents come to all my sporting events whether I'm doing well or not. They always think I'm the best!*

In a similar vein, I recently asked a group of kids — teenagers and collegians — to tell me an example of something their parents have done that expressed love to them. What a heart-warming (and heart-instructing) list their answers make:

- *Mom made doll clothes for my doll.*
- *Dad makes sure I have enough food to eat at college; when he comes to visit, he takes me grocery shopping.*
- *Mom drew cartoons on my lunch bags, and put notes into them.*
- *Mom did surprise scavenger hunts after school (when it wasn't even a special occasion).*
- *When I'm playing music in my room, Dad comes in and two-steps with me.*
- *When I was a kid, Dad kept the lawn mowers in good repair so I could mow lawns.*
- *My Daddy used to take me to work with him for the day, and show me off to his fellow workers.*
- *Mom used to let me jump on her bed.*

365 Ways to Tell Your Child "I LOVE YOU"

(continued)

115. Compliment your child's attempt to keep a tidy room.
116. The Bible's love chapter says that love "keeps no record of wrongs..." (1 Corinthians 13:5). Have you learned to let go of your child's past failures?
117. Show your child one of his baby pictures, and tell him why it's one of your favorites.

- *When I was little, my Dad let me drive the golf cart around while he played golf.*
- *If I had misbehaved with my friends in the yard, my parents never raised their voice when calling me into the house to discipline me. They'd talk to me, sometimes spank me, then give me time to regain my composure and wash my face before returning to play.*
- *While performing on stage at school, I looked out and saw my Daddy smile and give me a "thumbs up."*
- *My Dad played and coached baseball for thirteen years. When I began to pursue tennis, he quit baseball and began spending time coaching me in tennis.*
- *Whenever I use the family car, Dad fills it with gas and checks the oil and tires.*
- *My Mom colored pictures for me and mailed them to me at school.*
- *My Mom let my brother and me have a cat — and she hates cats.*
- *My parents gave me some strict rules (like not dating until I was sixteen, not going out on school nights, etc.) that helped make me a better person.*
- *Mom told me it's okay to disagree with her, that I'm my own person in Christ and my eyes should be on Him, not her.*
- *During finals week my Mom sends me something fun every day to keep me going.*

- *Dad came to school and ate lunch with me.*
- *When my Dad comes home from work, he immediately finds me and talks with me and asks how my day was.*
- *When I'm in a hurry before going out on a date, my mother would iron my clothes and dry my hair while I put on makeup.*
- *My Mom would wake me up in the morning by opening my curtains, singing to me, then asking me what I wanted for breakfast.*
- *My Dad is NEVER negative when he comes home from work.*
- *When we built snow forts to have snowball fights, Dad would let us have the awesome fort he built, and he would fight from the sorry one we built.*
- *Mom would eat the heels in a loaf of bread, because we didn't like them.*
- *When I wanted to look nice for a special occasion, my Mom would always offer me something nice of her own to wear, and it made me feel special.*
- *My Mom took me to gymnastics practice every day for five years. It was thirty miles away, and she would just wait around until I was through, and then take me back. She gave up her time for me.*
- *When we moved across town, my parents drove me back every day so I could stay in the same school with my friends.*

365 Ways to Tell Your Child **"I LOVE YOU"**

(continued)

118. Help your daughter fix her hair in a special way.
119. Take a winter's afternoon off and put a jigsaw puzzle together.
120. Make your child's favorite cookies or snack for him.
121. Ask your child — with genuine and obvious sincerity — how his day was.

- *My Dad told me every day, "I love you more today than I did yesterday."*
- *The day I graduated from high school, my Mom gave me four big scrapbooks, one for each year of high school. She had clipped and saved items on everything I'd ever done, without my even knowing about it.*
- *When I was four years old, my Mom and I found a maple tree seed just beginning to grow in the ground, and we transplanted it. Ever since it's been referred to as my tree.*

NOT SO SPECIAL

TEARS FILLED HER BLUE EYES as she spoke candidly about her father:

"He never asked me to go with him or to do anything with him just so he could spend time with me....He had a lot of time for hunting or things that were special to him, but I wasn't one of those things. That thought hurt a lot when I was younger. Now that I'm older, it hurts even more."

These words — from a twenty-year-old loaded with beauty and wealth — accurately reflect our kids' real desires.

365 Ways to Tell Your Child **"I LOVE YOU"**

(continued)

122. Occasionally include your son or daughter when doing something with your adult friends.
123. Take your child out to breakfast (just you and him) before school.
124. For a temporary but fun change in your home's decor, cover a wall with paper (a roll of "butcher's wrap" is great for this),

365 Ways to Tell Your Child *"I LOVE YOU"*

(continued)

then work together to "make a big scene" using colored markers or poster paint. Add into your artwork some "I love you" messages to your child.

125. Before a big event in your child's life — a birthday, a competition, a big test at school — decorate his room with crepe paper and posters.

FIRSTS

IT'S ALMOST MIDNIGHT. I just finished cleaning six doves that my son Brady shot this afternoon. They're now tucked away in the freezer for Thanksgiving Day.

My brothers and I grew up hunting with our Daddy, and we always ate what we killed. But the best part of it all was simply spending time with Daddy.

Now I'm the daddy, and the birds are Brady's. Yep, my boy shot 'em — some out of the air, some perched — all by himself, at age ten! This was a big first for him.

Am I a proud Papa, you ask? *Are you kiddin'?*

As I watched Brady walk across the freshly harvested cornfields at sunset, I saw his head held high. His face beamed with accomplishment.

And his Daddy was there. Oh, wow, was he ever!

There was another first in our family today. My six-year-old, Cooper, read his first billboard as we traveled to the dove hunt. As he carefully sounded out the words, I hugged him. A gold medal wouldn't have made a kid prouder.

There are thousands of firsts in the lives of every child. Each is a peak opportunity for encouragement. As the firsts have come in the lives of my children, I've learned that my place is at their side, cheering them on.

365 Ways to Tell Your Child *"I LOVE YOU"*

(continued)

126. Allow your child to plan the day for your family.
127. Send your child a fun balloon-o-gram at school.
128. In a relaxed time together, get out your high school or college yearbook and talk about your "school days" memories. (Be sensitive to focus on the things that your child seems most interested in).

When Brady learned to ride his bike I was too busy working hard. By the time my second son was ready, I had learned to work smarter (not harder). I pulled around that boy and his bike until my legs felt like concrete. But he and I still talk about how much fun that day was!

Besides first accomplishments, there are also those first defeats. A couple of nights ago I watched my oldest daughter and her team lose a squeaker in volleyball. As we walked to the car, I held my arm gently around her slightly drooping shoulders. It was a moment that knit my heart with hers...much like the moment when I held her, crying, after her first dog died...and the time I carried her to the doctor with her first serious injury...and the day I watched with tears as she got her first haircut, and baby-brown strands hit the hairdresser's floor.

Did any "firsts" happen in your family today?

Last night my best friend's son made his first interception while playing for his eighth-grade football team. His mom and dad were there.

Firsts. Don't miss those times:

First smile. First step. First "Ma-Ma." First dry diaper in the morning.

First tooth. First loose tooth.

First memorized Bible verse.

First somersault. First head stand. First bicycle ride. First dive in the pool. First time on skis.

First day at school. First school lunch. First book read.

First B average. First A. First straight A's.

First ribbon or trophy or medal.

First meal cooked.

First pet selection.

First home room office. First student council office.

First game of the season. First victory. First defeat. First letter jacket.

First party. First date.

First job. First paycheck.

First graduation. First goodbye when moving away from home.

PART TWO

FIRST THINGS FIRST

An Arm Up

I WATCH SO MANY KIDS who fail and then feel like failures. And I watch almost as many who *succeed* and then feel like failures. On a one-to-ten scale with ten being "I feel successful," I think kids across America have an average self-image of about 4.5.

The child who feels really good about himself — regardless of external beauty, quality of clothing, athletic success, or current popularity — seems to come around as rarely as Halley's Comet.

Austin Jones and Halley's Comet have a lot in common. Austin is one of my five thousand kids (at camp). His twinkling smile and galaxy of humble confidence set him further apart from the rest of my summer kids than does his left arm that quit developing just below the elbow. Austin can beat you at tennis, wipe you out in soccer, pitch a no-hitter in baseball, and melt you into nothing with his smile.

Austin's secret?

You guessed it.

Austin has a mom and dad who on day one began making him feel like a champion (not just "normal" — but a *champion!*). I'm sure insults and sneers were waiting at every corner, but Austin's ears were so filled with "You can do it, Buddy" and "Way to go, Austin — we're so proud of you" and "I wouldn't trade you for any kid in the world," that Austin never heard the "You'll never make it" or "A one-arm kid could never do that."

Austin's parents are my heroes. They're what today's power-success craze is missing!

Every Olympics fan has a favorite memory from a past Olympics event. I have two. One of them is about another young man who, like little Austin, had one deformed arm.

365 Ways to Tell Your Child **"I LOVE YOU"**

(continued)

129. Have fun together answering this question: If you were a brilliant scientist, what new process or product would you like most to invent?
130. The Bible's love chapter says that love "always protects…" (1 Corinthians 13:7). Think of a new and positive way you can truly offer *protection* to your child.

But that didn't keep baseball pitcher Jim Abbott from capturing America's heart in the 1988 Olympics in Seoul, as he went the distance in the final game to win the baseball gold medal for the United States. His name will be in my personal hall of fame forever. In the Korean sunlight that day, the only thing shining more brightly than Jim Abbott's gold medal was his smile — reflecting a triumphant legacy of overcoming the odds through courage implanted by parents. With every note of *The Star-Spangled Banner* that drew his fellow Americans to their feet that day, the message sounding to the world was that hope-building is a stronger motivation than any payoff, fringe incentive, or governmental pressure.

Going back further, my other favorite Olympic memory was being in the stands in 1972 in Munich and watching my dear friend, runner Jim Ryan, trip over his life's dream and miss the gold medal he had deserved for the fifteen years he was a world-record holder. Jim didn't stay down. He's still running — not to prove anything, or to inflate his ego; Jim never needed that. He runs to share his smile, his zest for life, and his deep faith in the eternal gold.

First Things First

JIM RYAN'S PARENTS gave him gold medal talent. My DNA code couldn't afford that for our foursome. They got so much of their daddy's flatness of feet, slowness, and all-around mediocrity of body that in their early sports

365 Ways to Tell Your Child *"I LOVE YOU"*

(continued)

131. Take your child out for a $20 or $30 after-school shopping spree.
132. Buy a guidebook to the trees and wild plants of your region, and take a nature hike to identify as many different kinds as you can. Take a notepad along to list your discoveries.
133. Go on a bike ride around the neighborhood together.

experiences they seldom even made the team. "B team," "the bench," and "honorable mention" were many of their early accolades.

Our kids' earliest IQ's looked pretty average as well. Again the genetic code gave them a lot of Daddy. Their mom made nearly all A's in college, but I struggled for B's and C's.

But what I didn't have to pass along in intellectual and athletic keenness, I did have in the encouragement and biblical foundation that my parents gave me. So when our kids were born, Debbie Jo and I began to discuss and develop and pray for our family priorities. We decided that although I enjoyed football, becoming a starter (or even playing) was at the bottom of the list of what we would emphasize to our kids. Being a cheerleader or homecoming queen were down on the same level. Becoming valedictorian wasn't going to be stressed. In each area, making the "first team" just wouldn't be the focus.

Instead, we wanted our kids — who were quite average at birth — to grow most of all in these directions:

❶ Knowing they have a mom and dad who love each other, and who are committed to God and the family.

❷ Having a deep, abiding, personal walk with Christ.

❸ Memorizing the Bible by chapters and books (by doing it verse by verse, day by day).

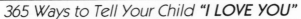

4. Being involved in some sort of physical fitness training (of their own choosing) year round.
5. Maintaining a standard of purity in our lifestyle at home. No immoral or even "gray area" TV programs, music, movies, magazines, books, etc., in our home or in our private lives (this goes for parents as well as kids).
6. Having lots of creative fun and recreation together — we'd focus on "getting our good times together" as a *family*.
7. Having solid friendships.
8. Having a "never quit" commitment to integrity and morals.

(Now we're getting to the bottom of the list.)

9. Getting good grades at school — "Be the best you can be."
10. Having well-rounded hobbies — in music, art, sports, and so on.

Funny things have happened in the last couple of years. The kids are making almost all A's. (The Bible promises that if a kid is taught to memorize and meditate on Scripture, he'll be blessed. And recent scientific studies

365 Ways to Tell Your Child ***"I LOVE YOU"***

(continued)

134. Take your child out for bowling or miniature golf, and dinner afterwards.
135. Write your child a short poem and stick it in his pocket or lunch box before school.
136. Honor your child with a "just because" party ("just because I love you") and invite over his friends.

show that improved study and retention skills can result directly from regular Bible memory work.) Courtney has won the state championship in gymnastics, Jamie is a starter for her volleyball team, Brady won his school's physical fitness award, and Cooper just smiles at it all (he's just getting started).

Honestly, they all started off slowly.

Courtney is especially sensitive and sweet today, but she began her earthly stay as the typical strong-willed second child screaming her way through life. When doing a *Focus on the Family* radio show with Dr. James Dobson two years ago, he asked me if strong-willed babies became strong-willed teens. I thought the answer was yes, but thanks to reading his books (which Debbie Jo and I devoured) and a "first things first" approach in our home, Courtney broke the stereotype.

I watch parents who scream at their kids' coaches and referees (in PeeWee football, of all places), and scream at their bewildered children as well. I've seen parents make kids feel bad for a getting a "C" on a test, or make fun of the zits on their kids' faces. I've seen parents put earrings on two-year-olds and makeup on sixth-graders. And yet these poor boys and girls have a growing insecurity, and they couldn't tell you a passage of Scripture or convey any warmth about their relationship with the Lord to save their lives.

If your main goal is to have your son become a Friday-night football hero, a popular school leader, or a highly

365 Ways to Tell Your Child ***"I LOVE YOU"***

(continued)

137. Prepare a special dessert that's just for your child.
138. Have a family slumber party in the family room in front of the fireplace (complete with treats and old-movie videos on TV).
139. Buy a children's crossword puzzle book, and do one puzzle together each night until you complete the book.

365 Ways to Tell Your Child *"I LOVE YOU"*

(continued)

140. Pretend you're a team of movie producers, and plan out together the plot and scenes for your next production.
141. Plan a family scavenger hunt around the house, with prizes for all.
142. Cut out pictures from magazines, and make a collage illustrating your child's talents, interests, and favorite activities.

paid executive in the future — I'll probably be seeing him in my counseling office someday. If, to meet your approval, your daughter must be slender, attractive, and perfectly poised, plus be either a straight-A student or a skilled athlete, musician, or artist, she'll probably never make it to my office; an abortion clinic or a hospital's suicide ward or anorexia treatment center will get to her first.

Do you wonder why one of seven teens each year try suicide? Why thirty percent of all sorority girls have eating disorders? Why forty percent of today's teenage girls will become pregnant while still in their teens — with almost half of those ending up with abortion scars?

Listen to what we're telling our kids:

"Why don't you lose a couple of pounds this month?"

"Bill, if you could just quit riding that bench..."

"Honey, why don't you try this new makeup brand?"

"Those eyelashes really look great today."

"Hey, if you want a tennis racket, get yourself a job."

EIGHTEEN FLEETING YEARS

PRIORITIES.

What is *really* important?

When your son or daughter is forty-one, with friends who are leaving sanity and family behind for a hot car, a

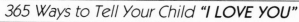

365 Ways to Tell Your Child **"I LOVE YOU"**

(continued)

143. Dry and brush your child's hair after a shower, and have a neat chat while you're doing it.
144. With an Etch-a-Sketch toy, do a "silent partners" drawing together: Take turns adding a single line to the drawing, but don't tell one another what you're trying to draw. See what you come up with!

young flame, a more lucrative career — what then will you wish you had given him or her *today?*

A few years from now, when your child is sixteen and comes home from the abortion clinic or the drug rehab program or an overnight in jail — what then will you wish your priorities had been *today?*

Dave came to our camp for six summers. He was the most delightful fourteen-year-old I'd ever known. His mom and dad were wonderful.

Then a little racial unrest developed at Dave's school. His parents couldn't resist the urge to "send him off for a better education" (one of his friends had gone to an expensive boarding school in the East and had come home with much higher test scores).

I talked with his parents about the importance of spending those high school years in the home; developing spiritual values and deepening family ties are such greater priorities than education. But I reasoned to no avail.

Dave went. He drifted spiritually. He drifted from the family. The negative changes that year in his life and the family's life may never be recouped.

I've seen the same scenario repeatedly. If first things aren't first, it's impossible to convince an ambitious mom or dad that this tragic decline can happen to their family, too.

The Bible exhorts us, "Lean not on your own understanding, but in all your ways acknowledge Him (and His Word)." We all blow that great command as we naively stumble through our childhood — but when we're old enough to know better, it's tragic to deviate so much from God's plan in carrying out our responsibilities for our kids. (The Bible tells parents clearly to "train" our kids, and to "bring up your children in the discipline of the Lord.")

When I was on a college football coaching staff, the coaches met every day at 9 A.M. to prioritize and strategize our precious 120 minutes on the practice field. In our summer camp today, the staff also meets daily for the same purpose.

But how often do you and your spouse meet to plan and pray for those priceless, fleeting eighteen years of your child's development? (If you're a single parent, the planning job can still be accomplished well with pen and paper and the Spirit of God in your heart to "guide you into all truth.")

YELLOW LIGHTS

"WHERE ARE YOU GOING tonight, Jamie, dear?"

"Oh, my friends and I are going out."

"What do you and your friends have planned, Sweetie?"

"Whatever."

365 Ways to Tell Your Child **"I LOVE YOU"**

(continued)

145. Always display (on the refrigerator or in another prominent spot) the artwork or other creations your child made at school, Sunday school, etc.
146. The Bible's love chapter says that love "always trusts…" (1 Corinthians 13:7). Think of a specific way you can grow in *trusting* your child.

Do you ever feel the depth gauge on conversations with your children measures only about a millimeter?

"What did you and your friends do tonight, Brady?"

"Good grief, Dad, what are you, some kind of reporter or something?"

Do you see the warning sign when a conversation with your child goes like that?

Red lights — signals indicating that danger has arrived — are easy to spot. They come with a crash to many parents of teenagers: a call from the police station, or the discovery in a blue jeans pocket of drug paraphernalia, or a birth control prescription. You can't miss those.

But the skilled parent is one who notices when the light first goes from green to yellow — the warning signal.

"Who did you go with tonight, Son?"

"Well, you know, friends. Like, I mean — you know, Dad."

Conversations at dinner can be so painful during those high school years. Dad works all day (and maybe Mom, too) to bring home the bacon. Mom works like crazy preparing it into a feast. As the kids sit down to the table and groan, their parents — both near emotional exhaus-

365 Ways to Tell Your Child ***"I LOVE YOU"***

(continued)

147. Say "Please" and "Thank you" each time you ask your child to do something.
148. Let the kids sleep in your bed with you when your spouse is out of town. (You may not get much sleep, but they'll remember it forever.)
149. Reward your son or daughter for getting good grades.

365 Ways to Tell Your Child *"I LOVE YOU"*

(continued)

150. While you're driving your child somewhere, hold his or her hand, and squeeze it.
151. Tell your spouse how proud you are of your child for something he did (and let him overhear your remarks).
152. As you notice your child making or doing something creative, call other family members to come and see.

tion — have to buy a look of acknowledgment that they're even in the room.

"How was school today, Hon?"

"Fine."

"What did you and your friends do after classes?"

"Oh, just some stuff. You know, Dad, stuff like that."

If they wanted you in their world, they would tell you about it — that is, if they thought you'd really listen and if they knew you *really* cared. But when the answers get short and mysterious, you've got yellow lights.

"Hey, kids, your Dad and I are planning a wonderful trip for all of us this weekend!"

"Not again?"

"Count me out."

"Me, too."

When your children are into family things — when they can't wait to spend time with you tonight or on the weekend or over spring break — the light is green. When their interest sags...open your eyes to the yellow warning.

A teacher tells you: "Andrea doesn't pay attention in class anymore. She's drifting."

Your wife says, "Honey, I just can't get Julie up in the morning. I didn't know being sixteen could be so exhausting."

Your child says, "Dad, I don't want to study tonight. Grades just aren't that important to me."

Or, "It's none of your business who my friends are, Mom. What are you trying to do, interrogate me?"

You find yourself saying, "You need to pay attention when I talk to you. I won't keep repeating myself three times every time we talk."

Or, "Baby, you ought to at least try out for Pep Club this year. You didn't want to be a cheerleader or on the track team...it seems like school is boring you this year."

The yellow lights are flashing throughout America's homes — and few moms and dads are doing anything about them.

Excessive sleep... lack of motivation... negative comments about teachers, coaches, and other authorities... slipping grades... cutting class... evasive answers... exaggerated answers... short, spacy, meaningless answers... a sudden change of friends... radical hairstyle, makeup, and jewelry... silence at home... obvious efforts to stay away from home as much as possible... negligence in fulfilling responsibilities — all these are warning signals.

Just a block from my house, eighteen teenagers live in a group home for youths from reconstructing families. In the past eight years, approximately one hundred young lives have been retooled through spending a year or so in the home. When their parents first called us, red lights were flashing everywhere, and couldn't be ignored. These

365 Ways to Tell Your Child ***"I LOVE YOU"***

(continued)

153. Make a special greeting card for your child that in your own handwriting says "I Love You" in as many different languages as you can find the words for. (You'll probably need a trip to the library for this one!)
154. Give your child a hug when he's feeling down.
155. When your child is sick, stay up with him at night.

365 Ways to Tell Your Child "I LOVE YOU"

(continued)

156. Discuss together this question: If you were asked to appear before Congress to tell what three new laws you think our country needs most, what would you say?
157. A fun and challenging project to do together: Draw and color a map of your house. Do your best to draw it to correct scale.

moms and dads used the words "desperate," "runaway," "hospital," "urgent," "broken." They were crying out for help: "There's nothing we can do anymore...we seem to have lost all hope."

All these teenagers (and I mean *all*) are truly neat kids. In time, most of them do very well. But the phase in which reconstruction must begin for them and their families is extremely difficult for all concerned. Lots and lots and lots of hurt prevails.

My dream wish is that this youth home and others like them would be put out of business...because no red lights had flashed...because parents had been alert and acted skillfully when the lights first turned yellow. What a wonderful indication that would be for America's future.

Green-light days are the time for fun, for easy closeness, for family campouts and hunting trips, for marshmallows roasted by the fireplace, for smiles and prayers together at bedtime. Those moments are so special. You can't get enough of 'em. How I cherish every one!

Yellow-light days are something else. Everything looks different. We feel swarmed by new and stressful emotions.

Don't run yellow lights! Slow down, and embrace those days. When they come, if you can digest, discuss, and pray through the following procedures I've listed, there's a good chance our youth home director will never get a phone call from you.

365 Ways to Tell Your Child "I LOVE YOU"

(continued)

158. Take sack lunches for you and your child, and enjoy them together at a local park.
159. Volunteer to give your daughter a perm, or to help fix her hair in some other way.
160. Smile when you're together, and be ready to laugh when your child does.

✚ Love your child while you hate his sin. Draw in close. Let him know (repeatedly) that nothing he could ever do could endanger your love for him and your commitment to him. Your son's drugs and your daughter's boyfriend will eventually let them down — but be sure they know *you won't.*

✚ Quietly gather evidence. Know what your kids are doing. Knowing what's going on will help you talk with intelligence rather than assumption. Don't rely only on what your son or daughter tells you. Lying is a way of life for kids in the yellow-light zone, and parents are usually the most easily fooled.

"Don't you trust me?" your son protests. "Yes," you affirm, "But it's a much deeper issue than that. I *believe* in you. I believe in *you.* What I don't trust is the insurmountable peer pressure that you and other kids are put under today — the pressure that has ninety percent of all high school seniors drinking and eighty-two percent of the boys having sex...while a hundred percent wish they had parents bold enough to blow the whistle. So, Buddy, we're in this one together."

If there's a joint in his pants pocket, I hope you find it. If there's a sex note in her drawer, I hope you read it before you suddenly receive an invoice from an abortion clinic.

✚ Be firm (but not outrageous). Kids want to be rescued from their sin. Nobody likes sin. But the drive for acceptance among adolescents is stronger than gravity.

When my kids begin to stray, I have a meeting with them. I don't scream or make giant threats; we just quietly discuss the problem and describe the action to be taken if things don't change. If they're being selfish, we don't eat the next meal until we begin serving each other. If they're ungrateful or disrespectful or disobedient, we don't nag at them; we just tell them eyeball-to-eyeball about the privileges they've lost until attitude changes have been made. Their mom and I work hard to pay for things like gasoline and a telephone. In order to get to use them, the kids work hard on their attitudes.

I'm amazed how much abuse parents allow from their kids! Letting kids get away with bad behavior is detrimental to their character, and it's also especially damaging to mothers. An old sea captain told me that when he was seventeen his mother said to him, "When you were young, you stepped on my toes. Now you step on my heart."

✚ Examine yourself carefully. Kids have wonderful radar systems called "baloney detectors." Are you and your spouse being genuine as you convey appreciation, respect, and support? If you aren't, your kids will spot it — and follow the trend.

365 Ways to Tell Your Child ***"I LOVE YOU"***

(continued)

161. When your child is upset or hurt, make *listening* your first response.
162. The Bible's love chapter says that love "always hopes…" (1 Corinthians 13:7). Are you keeping in mind an exciting view of your child's greatest potential? Think of a way you can grow in your *hope* for your child.

When lights are yellow in your home, stand in God's Word, and stand together with your spouse. If you're fighting it alone as a single parent, be sure your lifestyle is in line with Scripture.

There's a giant difference between yellow lights in the home and those out on the street, and that difference is a source of endless hope: With the right measure of parental alertness and wisdom and love, the yellow lights at home can change back to green instead of turning red.

HOPE STEALERS

PAUL HARVEY HAS SAID that ninety percent of all the news we hear is bad news. Psychologists say that over eighty percent of the things we say to ourselves about ourselves is negative. And for some crazy reason, I find that no more than ten percent of all the peer pressure our kids face today is positive.

Most of the rock music poured at the unquenchable thirst of America's youth is not just negative — it's depressing. Every kid I've ever met who was on drugs was also into heavy-metal or related rock music. Every one of the bizarre, satanic teen murders that are becoming more prevalent are connected to heavy-metal music. I've personally observed hundreds of teenagers who've gone through drastic changes in very short periods of time under the influence of contemporary rock music. I believe

365 Ways to Tell Your Child ***"I LOVE YOU"***

(continued)

163. Plant flower or vegetable seeds with your child. As over time you together see the plants sprout and grow, use the opportunity to talk about your child's growth — physically, intellectually, socially, and spiritually.
164. Go shopping for clothes together.
165. Talk together about what you believe about God.

365 Ways to Tell Your Child **"I LOVE YOU"**

(continued)

166. With help from friends and others in the family, prepare a "This Is Your Life" skit to honor your child on a special occasion.
167. With your child, talk openly about your most significant convictions, and ask for his opinions in response.
168. Kiss your young child's hurt when he falls down.

it's the most dangerous and devastating influence a society has ever unleashed on its young people.

Most parents don't take the time to understand rock music's message, and don't have the courage to say, "No, we don't allow sexual perverts in this house, nor do we allow in those who put their perversion to music. We don't allow drug pushers in the house, nor do we allow in those who push drugs into your subconscious."

Hope stealers.

Keep them out of your kids' lives!

Who is responsible to filter the countless thousands of suggestions of premarital sex that the average teen receives in entertainment media? Mom and Dad are responsible.

Is it hard to carry out that responsibility? It's war at times! But in the deepest crevices of their hearts, kids *want* to be guided.

The task is hardest when some of your close friends let their kids watch questionable movies or TV programs. I believe the only way you can succeed is this: *Stay close to your kids, make them feel like a billion bucks, and make your home the funnest place on this earth to be.*

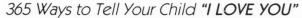

365 Ways to Tell Your Child "I LOVE YOU"

(continued)

169. In a relaxed moment together, talk about favorite memories from the past (even younger children enjoy this — their "past" may be short in years, but relative to their ages it seems just as long as ours). Talk about favorite gifts, favorite toys, favorite surprises.
170. Build and fly kites together.

Author and radio personality Earl Nightingale said that the only fact in psychology that all mind-scientists have agreed on is this: "You become what you think about." (Solomon in his Proverbs said it first: "As a man thinketh in his heart, so is he.") And we think about what we see and hear. As one psychologist has said, "A person can be taught to believe anything if he hears it enough times."

Every kid is susceptible to whoever encourages him the most. If he's encouraged by the bands AC/DC and Motley Crue, you can expect him to have dark, violent, perverted thoughts. If he is encouraged by God's Word and by his parents' genuine modeling of that Word in their love and behavior, it will lead a child into an ear-to-ear grin of goodness.

I'm convinced that young boys who have sexual dreams and find the need to masturbate and think lust-filled thoughts when girls walk by have been encouraged to begin formulating frustrated sexual innuendos in their minds, and the encouragement comes not only from rock music, but also from movies, television, and magazines.

So who's encouraging your kids the most these days?

Hope thieves aren't sneaky. You can see the evidence of them everywhere. On television, for example, the warning signs flash in cartoons full of evil symbolism...prime time commercials laced with sexual attention grabbers...depressive, violent, sexually blatant scenes on MTV... soaps and sit-coms in which more than ninety percent of all reference to sex is outside of marriage... H.B.O. offerings, of which less than ten percent are obviously suitable for children. All are stealing hope from your kids.

Music recordings don't hide their crime, either. Look at the symbols on the album or tape or CD covers — besides sexually suggestive illustrations, signs of evil are everywhere: pentagrams, skull and crossbones, the mark of the beast, sacrificial altars, tarot cards, goat heads. For your easy examination, the product's packaging usually includes the printed lyrics for most of the songs — which typically range from suggestive to incredibly repulsive.

Think of the movies you see. A PG-rated film has an average of five to ten four-letter words, and the dialogue will include the Lord's name taken in vain at least twice. A typical PG-13 movie will include scenes of immoral sex and violence, and even more offensive language.

So when hope thieves enter our homes, we are without excuse.

Think how bizarre and foolish it would it be to go to the bank, take out your life savings in cash, stack the money on your dining room table, invite over any criminals you could contact, open your front door, then leave home for a week. Last time I checked, my child's soul is infinitely more valuable than our savings account.

*365 Ways to Tell Your Child **"I LOVE YOU"***

(continued)

171. Always welcome your child's friends to your home, and practice hospitality toward them.
172. Roast some nuts together, then shell and eat them together by the fire.
173. Say to your child, "Let's spend some time together, just you and me."

Right now in our family, none of us watch more than a select few TV shows. We go to only two or three movies annually. We listen to only Christian music, or (rarely) approved secular music.

Are we square? Yes.

Legalistic? No.

The hours during which our kids are *not* watching TV or movies or listening to radio rock music, we fill with hunting trips, canoe trips, sports activities, family games, "mystery" trips of all types, kite flying, rocket building, and whatever else seems impulsive, zany, and memorable.

THE FEAR FACTOR

THE LETTERS I RECEIVE from teens often scream with fear:

> Every time I do something wrong my Mom freaks out, starts yelling at me like I'm a two-year-old. I'm afraid to be around her anymore.
>
> (from a sixteen-year-old)

> My Dad actually scares me to death. I never know when he is going to hit me next. I don't know how to make him happy with me.
>
> (from a fourteen-year-old)

365 Ways to Tell Your Child **"I LOVE YOU"**

(continued)

174. Give your child positive nicknames. (In our house we've used "Super Cooper," "Little Buddy," "Rocky-Pop," etc.)
175. *Listen* to your child with "unconditional ears."
176. The Bible's love chapter says that love "always perseveres…" (1 Corinthians 13:7). Commit yourself today to *never let up* in your love for your child. Keep going and growing!

365 Ways to Tell Your Child "I LOVE YOU"

(continued)

177. Give your child the freedom to fail. Remember, mistakes are never fatal.
178. Encourage your child often to be himself. Tell him, "I like you for who you are."
179. Tell your son or daughter, "I'll never give up on you."
180. Write a funny poem — the crazier the better — to your child.

In the book of First John, the antithesis of fear is proclaimed on a billboard, as God's encouraging sign to remind us every time we pass by: "Perfect love casts out fear."

I fear lakes and swimming pools, a fear reinforced by vivid memories: of the time when I was five, and saw the waters of our friend's pool close over my head, as I sank desperately to the bottom...and of a time years later, when I searched for my young friend, Ricky, who had just disappeared under a lake's dark surface. These scenes have engraved a horror in my subconscious which I've never completely overcome.

As strong as the fear is, however, there are few things I enjoy more than teaching my kids to water ski or to swim or to catch a two-pound rainbow trout from the Ozark lake in front of our house.

Tiny scars dot the backs of the hands of all of us who've enjoyed chef's duty over an open fire on family cookouts. Nothing burns worse than hot grease — but, boy, aren't those outdoor-flavored meals the greatest!

As cold darkness descended on the Breckenridge, Colorado, ski slopes, a frantic search for my son Brady in nearby dense woods was a father's nightmare! But how we celebrated when the search was successful — and how we thrilled ourselves the next day, swooshing freely down those same slopes.

Great events almost always have a link with great fears.

365 Ways to Tell Your Child *"I LOVE YOU"*

(continued)

181. In a relaxed moment together with your child, ask, "What do you think is the most challenging thing you've ever accomplished?"
182. Be honest. If you have wrongly withheld or distorted something in the way you've talked with your child, confess your dishonesty and tell your child the truth.

I fear the awesome. I fear God...and there is nothing or no one on this earth whom I love-respect more than I do Him. It makes me tremble to think of His penalty for ignoring His love-motivated, sacrificial gift of salvation. Appreciating and enjoying a personal relationship with Him brings me deep-rooted happiness beyond description.

There is a fairness about God that turns the fear into love. There is a "He loved us first" quality about God that turns the fear into respect. There is an "I'll wash your feet" serving quality about God's Fatherhood that turns the fear into reverence. There is an unconditional acceptance about God that turns fear into worship. There is a "forgiving to the point of forgetting" ability about God that turns my fear into tears of gratitude. There is a bleeding-sacrifice quality about God's nature that turns my fear into allegiance.

There is also a firmness with God, an exactness, an expression of "If you don't do as I command you to do, you're going to have problems every time." Yet this quality about God only deepens my respect, deepens my love, and deepens my awe and reverence for Him.

An earthly parent should develop this same kind of "fear" in the heart of his child.

The right fear is fun. The right fear is freedom. The right fear is firm. The right fear is fantastic.

Most of all, the right fear is necessary.

Ten-year-old Brady is all boy. He's spontaneous, wonderful, sometimes selfish, gentle, sweet. Like all other boys, he needs the loving hand of discipline. Last summer we were having a rich discussion of his favorite things in life. I asked him what he liked best about his mom. He said, "She's firm" (not, "mean," but "firm").

He was right. Debbie Jo puts up strong boundaries. Spankings are seldom, but given when needed. She never allowed whiny, gripy, spoiled kids. Her husband supports her to the max. We back each other up, and any disrespectful words or actions get dealt with from both of us.

As I drove my two girls on a father-daughter outing last week, I commented cheerfully about how many great times the three of us had shared in the past six months. With confidence, and without knowing what was around the corner, I said, "I'd say this has been a great year for our relationship, hasn't it, girls?" Super-honest Courtney looked at me respectfully and returned, "Well, let's say we've gotten to know each other better this year."

I chuckled to myself as I reflected back over the wonderful adolescent growing pains we had been wading through all year — phone calls from boys, movies, parties, makeup, pierced ears, going steady, etc. We're a lot more strict than many other parents, but Debbie Jo and I charge through this jungle of uncertainties boldly together.

Yes, in our family we've gotten to know each other better this year! We've had challenges, and times when

365 Ways to Tell Your Child ***"I LOVE YOU"***

(continued)

183. Share your life with your child; let him into your world. Tell him the things you like most about your life and work, and talk together about some of the frustrations as well. Talk about your hopes and dreams in every area of your life.
184. When you and your child are around other adults, include him in your conversations with them.

our parental policies needed careful explanation. But instead of half-spoiled daughters who are ooey-gooey in love with me today because of my permissiveness, I'd prefer having daughters who are head-over-heels crazy about me — and grateful for the way I've chosen to father them — on the day they put on a white wedding gown.

And remember: The right "fear" and the wrong one — being "scared" — are two totally different concepts when it comes to moms and dads.

Scared kids get hit with the back of the hand. Scared kids get yelled at. Scared kids get impulsive discipline without loads of thoughtful love. Scared kids are surrounded by giant walls of rules and punishment that have no foundation of encouragement and concern.

A relationship in which kids rightly fear (respect) their parents is like good driving on a well-designed mountain highway. The boundaries are there for sure — well-posted speed limits and warning signs, guard rails, and banked curves — but by staying in the boundaries everyone enjoys a wonderful world of scenery and a smooth journey.

365 Ways to Tell Your Child ***"I LOVE YOU"***

(continued)

185. Buy a pack of chewing gum to give to your child — but first slip a tiny note inside the outer wrapper of each piece. In each note, list one of the qualities of your child that you most admire: "I love you because you're so ________."
186. Without being preachy, talk openly with your child about the dangers of substance abuse.

365 Ways to Tell Your Child ***"I LOVE YOU"***

(continued)

187. On your child's birthday, prepare your own greeting card with a poem to your child.
188. Leave a note of encouragement inside your child's favorite pair of shoes.
189. As often as possible, let your child hear you tell your spouse, "I love you."

ADOLESCENT SPECIALTY

"LOOK OUT WORLD," you hear them saying, "here I come!"

✗ ✗ ✗

✗ She's five feet, four inches tall, too young to drive and too old to bike, too young to date and too old to stay home on Saturday night, too young for makeup and too old to go out with pimples, too young for panty hose and too old for bobbie socks.

✗ Along with a combination of apathetic grunts and early morning groans, his vocabulary consists mainly of "like you know," "sorta like," "I dunno," "I'm not sure," "don't bug me," "maybe," "whatever," "not me," and "but you said..."

✗ What her parents say doesn't matter much anymore, because they're out of it. And what God says is irrelevant because He doesn't understand anyway.

✗ One of his friends came over the other night with a few pictures ripped out of a *Playboy,* and opened up to him the confusing world of hormones and masturbation.

✗ She grapples with questions like "Why do people kiss on television in new car commercials in bathtubs?" "What's this twenty-eight-day cycle all about?" "Why won't

365 Ways to Tell Your Child *"I LOVE YOU"*

(continued)

190. Talk frequently with your child about spiritual lessons you're learning. (Invite his observations about how well you're learning them.)
191. During an enjoyable time when you're talking together, ask your child, "What are the most important decisions you've ever made?"

Jim pay attention to me anymore?" "How close should I dance at the school party?"

✗ The air in your home is filled with statements like, "You'd better accept me as I am or not at all." "You're always on my case." "You bug me."

✗ Today she's seated happily on a cloud. Tomorrow she's hidden miserably behind the eight ball.

✗ One of the kids in his school committed suicide three months ago. And one of his closer friends tried to take that dead-end street just last week.

✗ At school, if she says something nice about a teacher or her mom's cooking, everyone looks at her like she's crazy. Nobody seems to think dads are very worthwhile, either.

✗ At a party he went to at a friend's house, the parents accidentally-on-purpose left beer out. He wondered why something that tasted so bad could make everyone so happy. Two of his friends got drunk. He's totally confused.

✗ She constantly nagged her mom until she bought her the kind of outfits her friend Shannon wears; but now Shannon's look is out of style.

✗ One day he wants new jeans; the next day at school he feels like a geek because they don't have giant rips in the knees.

✗ Her new definition of *heaven* is a second look and a love note from a cute boy in third-hour English.

✗ The 7 A.M. chip on his shoulder has become the only consistent style of daily dress in town.

✗ His parents say sex is for married people, but the only married people he knows insult each other a lot. TV and the movies make sex look so intriguing, without even a passing reference (unless it's a negative one) to any need for marriage.

✗ If she's not going steady with someone, she's totally out of it. If she is going steady, her boyfriend expects her unquestionably to give in to his incredible surge of sexual energy.

✗ Suddenly, sitting by his parents in church isn't cool anymore. Those Bible storybooks are too childish, but standard Bibles have print too small, and the King James Version may as well be in Latin.

✗ She thought the only way she could get her parents' attention was to pretend to attempt suicide, so she slit her wrists. It worked so well that six of her friends are considering it today.

✗ ✗ ✗

Only four out of a hundred teens like their dads — and only half of all teens have a dad in their homes. Eighty-two percent of teens drink (almost all of them too much),

365 Ways to Tell Your Child ***"I LOVE YOU"***

(continued)

192. The Bible's love chapter says that "love never fails..." (1 Corinthians 13:8). In a quick but sincere prayer, thank God now that His love for both you and your child is everlasting, and ask Him to continue teaching you about love. Then think of a special way to tell your child today, *"I will always love you."*

and sixty percent have smoked pot. Eight out of ten agree with TV that sex outside marriage is okay. About one third of them have sex on their first date, or perhaps in an encounter a block away from school at lunch hour. High school kids today call it "scamming" — sex without any commitments. Seventy percent of high school kids are having sex, but only twenty-eight percent are actually "dating someone."

Adolescence. Was the old country lady right when she said with tongue in cheek, "When a boy is seventeen, he is the nothingest he ever is"? Did Mark Twain describe the right approach to adolescence by advising, "When your kid turns thirteen, put him in a barrel with nothing but a hole to feed him through; when he turns eighteen, plug the hole"?

I disagree — wholeheartedly.

I believe parenting teenagers is like snow-skiing on the steepest slopes, or playing Chopin on the piano, or baking an apple pie from scratch. It's a tremendous challenge, and you'd better work hard at it or you'll be blown away; but oh, the thrill of it!

It takes time, mental toughness, and diligent study. And yes, there's a great risk of disaster. But what a rush, as — like catching a giant wave on a surfboard off the west coast of Maui — you sail along, having successfully caught this great force of nature.

Teenagers — what incredibly rich and fun and gifted people they are.

365 Ways to Tell Your Child ***"I LOVE YOU"***

(continued)

193. Write a note of encouragement to your child, and pay to have it published in the classified ads section of your local newspaper.
194. Out of the blue, send your child a greeting card (either bought or homemade), and include a signed photograph of yourself.

365 Ways to Tell Your Child "I LOVE YOU"

(continued)

195. Prepare a dinner or lunch in which the name of every item served starts with the same letter as your child's first name (don't worry about whether it's a balanced meal). When your child asks the reason for the strange menu, let him guess.
196. Paint your fence together.

They want to be loved — *anyway.*
They want to be listened to — *every day.*
They want to be forgiven — *right away.*
They want to be free — *all the way.*
They want you to be there — *in work or play.*
They want Christ for an anchor at home — *to always stay.*
You'll guide them on your knees — *so forever pray.*

The eighteen teens who live away from their parents in our youth home grieve me — their parents are missing the greatest years of their lives.

I'll never forget "stealing" a watermelon with Mom and my brothers — then stumbling and breaking it wide open when Mom screamed that she saw Farmer Jones running toward me with a big dog. I cherish the years when Dad was there after I got wiped out in a football game, and when my Mom was there when my date stood me up. Those teenage hurts hurt a lot. Those mistakes still bring me pain at times. But what would I have done without those loving hands of my parents to tenderly cradle my searching heart?

If you dread your kids' adolescent years, it will be like never tasting the incomparable goodness of that homemade apple pie.

If you try to avoid them, it will be like always skiing on

197. If your child is sick in bed, read to him from his favorite books.
198. Make your child fortune cookies with notes of encouragement inside them.
199. Build a scarecrow together — whether you have a garden or not.

the flat, easy slopes, and never feeling the song of the wind whistling by your ears.

If you resist those roller-coaster years, it will be like never playing anything on the keyboard except Chopsticks.

Your kids' teen years can be your best days for creating scrapbook pages. Don't let them turn up blanks.

Celebrate your kids in their adolescence. Specialize in them. In your business or career, do what you must to keep plenty of time available for them. Get professional at saying "no" to all the wonderful outside-the-family opportunities that will pop up like mushrooms all around you during your kids' tender years. And learn to pray for your kids without ceasing.

Most of all, huddle up with each other as if you were about to line up to play in the Super Bowl. In that huddle, let God call your plays. Block for each other with sacrificial devotion.

When the adolescent game is over, you'll be able to carry your kids off the field on your shoulders, savoring the sweet taste of success. The tears will dry, the bruises will heal — and you'll all be more like the Savior for having fought the battle together.

Bury It!

WHEN IT COMES to the mystery of love, there is something so real about our Creator — and something so complete about His creation — that defies human understanding. The love He produces is as consistent as gravity and as miraculous as the tiny mechanism that sends the great Canada geese soaring thousands of miles across the continent in early spring to the exact spot where each one was hatched.

A man I know named Bud hasn't learned that yet. Or maybe he knows it, but his pride steps on his toes when he steps into the realm of God's designer laws.

Bud is forty-six and has three children, all nearly grown up and out of the house. They're great kids — Amy, Andy, and Sally — but one of them feels like a failure.

Amy and Andy feel good about themselves. Amy especially is the apple of her dad's eye. Being good at the right times always came easy for her. Bud can't remember when Amy's last discipline was.

But Sally's genetics didn't line up exactly like her sister's. (They never do.) Sally, it seems, has been blowing it consistently since her second birthday.

Now that she's a teenager I know her well, and she has a heart of gold. But her dad has convinced her it's made of coal. Every time she sees daylight and gets an edge on this

365 Ways to Tell Your Child ***"I LOVE YOU"***

(continued)

200. Buy your child a recording by his favorite performing artist (if you approve of the music).
201. Ask for your child's suggestions in planning your family vacation.
202. Go canoeing or rowing on a peaceful stream or lake — enjoy the peacefulness together.

thing we call success, Bud crunches her with reminders of how she used to hurt him when she would slip into sin.

Today Sally *really is* changing. Something new and wonderful is coming over that girl. And yet tonight Bud reopened the wound and sent that growing, emerging sprout of self-esteem (so tender and tenuous) back into the soil. How did he do it? By speculating out loud how short-lived Sally's new success pattern would be, and by reminding us about all her losing seasons in the past.

I had to confront him.

"Bud, you need to know I love you, but as a friend I've got to ask you to bury it."

"Bury what?!"

"Sally's past, man. You're wiping her out. She wants so badly to be approved by you like Amy is. She'd do anything to be Daddy's little girl, but she can't measure up to your standard of perfection."

His pridefulness swelled up within him. "You don't know how bad she's hurt me," he said. "I just can't let it happen again."

Bud's wife, Vicki, chimed in: "Well, she's been almost perfect for six months, Bud. I can't remember when she last made a mistake."

"Made a mistake!" I thought. *Good grief, I've made a hundred and fifty of them just today!* Did poor Sally have to be perfect to measure up? Had Bud forgotten about all the things he's been forgiven for? And where would we be

365 Ways to Tell Your Child ***"I LOVE YOU"***

(continued)

203. Enter together in a local race for amateur joggers.
204. *Listen* to your child, even when you don't feel like listening.
205. Hike up a mountain together.
206. Make it a special project today to *listen* intently to every word your child says.

365 Ways to Tell Your Child "I LOVE YOU"

(continued)

207. Attend every open-to-parents function at your child's school.
208. Get up early on a clear morning, find a quiet spot outdoors with a clear view to the east, and watch the sunrise together.
209. Talk frequently with your child about the truths in the Bible that you're enjoying in reading and meditation.

if *God* loved us only as long as we didn't mess up? Heaven would be as sparsely populated as a nuclear waste dump!

I'm surrounded by Sallys. They made an F on a test last semester. They cheated in ninth-grade Spanish class. They smoked dope. They lost their virginity on their fifteenth birthday, and you read about it in a note wadded up carelessly in a pair of jeans.

I was a Sally. I can't blame my parents, because it was a combination of a lot of my personal insecurities and mistakes. But, boy, is it hard to look into the mirror with any kind of dignity!

"There is therefore now no condemnation for those who are in Christ Jesus!" (Romans 8:1) If I condemn Sally, then I'm doing it alone — because God sure isn't.

Are you hanging on to any hurting remembrance of your child's failure?

Bury it, Mom and Dad! *Bury it!*

MORE FUNERALS NEEDED

HERE'S HOW TO CONDUCT a funeral service for bad memories about your kids:

First off all, pray about it *often.* One of the forces that's most destructive to my peace of mind toward those I love is bitterness and harbored hurt. It is devastating to me. If

365 Ways to Tell Your Child "I LOVE YOU"

(continued)

210. Sometime when you're enjoying being and talking together, ask your child, "In what area of life would you most like to improve in the next year?"
211. Go on a train or bus ride together.
212. Take up a new hobby or craft together — one that's new to both you and your child.

I never bring it before God (and keep it there), it will eat me up like cancer! I have to pray about it often, consistently, without ceasing. I take Jesus very seriously when He says, "Ask and you shall receive."

Next, put your child's failures (or those of whoever lets you down) at the foot of the Cross, right next to your own failures. It is amazing how level the ground is at the foot of the Cross. If God can accept me, as wretched as I am, how much more can He accept those who disappoint me?

Third, bathe your brain with Scripture. (Am I sounding like a broken record about getting the Word into your mind? I hope so!) The world says, "Get 'em back!" "Hit 'em first!" "Fight for your rights!" "Stand up and be counted!" But God's Word says, "As you forgive others, God will also forgive you." And, "No greater love has any man than to lay down his life (his pride, his harbored hurt) for his friends." As I memorize and meditate on God's Word my mind becomes conformed to His smile.

Finally, "8-1" the problem. Romans 8:1 says, "Therefore there is now no condemnation for those who are in Christ Jesus." That verse makes my heart do flip-flops inside — carnivals, parades, celebrations, fireworks! GOD DOESN'T CONDEMN ME! And if God doesn't condemn me, then He doesn't condemn my kids or my wife, even when they goof up royally! So when your pride is hurt, "8-1" it.

Then throw some dirt on it and plant flowers!

We need lots more funerals like that.

When Carol got pregnant she was only a sophomore in high school. Her Dad was vice-president of the local home-owned bank, and he sang in the church choir. Her mom was president of the PTA and led a women's Bible study group on Tuesday night. Carol's unexpected pregnancy took everyone by surprise. After the smoke cleared, however, and the months rolled by, Carol found out what fifteen years of "I love you's" truly meant. And when Carol's baby daughter was born, this fatherless child found herself securely in the arms of the most loving and accepting grandmom and granddad this earth has ever known.

Carol regrets her mistake, no doubt; but chances are she won't make it again. Like needle and thread, her mom's forgiveness and her dad's compassion have sown together her broken heart so well that you can hardly see where the rip used to be!

Carol loves herself again.

ONE SON'S STORY

ADOLPH COORS IV is a close friend who sits on my board of directors, and who has taken to heart many qualities that I admire. I suppose his finest quality surfaced as he came to grips with this difficult concept of forgiveness. On the pages that follow is his compelling story.

365 Ways to Tell Your Child "I LOVE YOU"

(continued)

213. Teach your child a special skill that you know (woodworking, needlepoint, etc.).
214. When your child shows particular interest in a national or world news item, talk about it together, discuss the media's presentation of it, and look at a map together to find the location.

"HATRED IS LIKE a rifle with a plugged barrel: The backfire is much more dangerous than the shot. Hating a person can be compared to burning down your house in order to kill a rat. And hatred once filled my heart so thoroughly, it literally consumed me.

"For seventeen long years I lived with the burden of anger and resentment towards the man who murdered my father, Adolph Coors III. I watched this hatred slowly eat away my mother, who steadily deteriorated over the last fifteen years of her life. This helped fuel my sense of helplessness and rage.

"My father was an extremely talented man. He earned a degree in chemical engineering from Cornell University. He was also a self-taught architect, and he designed and built the six-thousand-square-foot ranch home in Colorado that our family moved into when I was twelve.

"The one thing I remember most about my dad was the quality time he spent with me. He taught me how to hunt and fish and play baseball and ride a horse. Despite the job demands of being chairman of the board of the Adolph Coors Company, he always had time for my two older sisters, my younger brother, and me.

"My memories of life on our 476-acre ranch will always be special. Dad raised quarter horses, Angus beef cattle, and hay. My greatest joy was helping with the many chores that needed to be done, which enabled me to spend

365 Ways to Tell Your Child **"I LOVE YOU"**

(continued)

215. When you're watching TV together and see questionable scenes and dialogue presented, turn it off and talk together about what you find questionable and why.
216. Go to the library together and find all the information you can about one of your child's current interests — a hobby, a hero, a skill, or whatever.

365 Ways to Tell Your Child **"I LOVE YOU"**

(continued)

217. On an otherwise ordinary evening, serve the family dinner with candlelight and fancy place settings.
218. Review together the lyrics of the recordings that both you and your child own, or the songs you listen to on the radio, and talk about how honoring they are to God and how edifying they are to those who hear them.

time with this great man. We often rode together, enjoying the ranch's breathtaking scenery.

"You could say I idolized my dad. Yet I was to learn that one of the biggest mistakes anyone can make in life is to worship another human being. For then a problem arises: If your total trust is in an individual, what will you do if that person suddenly vanishes?

"That's how quickly Dad disappeared. The man who was the culprit had watched our home for hours, plotting how and when to kidnap him for ransom. One cold, February morning in 1960, in a matter of a few seconds, the crime was implemented.

"Dad had been trapped into thinking this man was a stranded motorist along the side of the road. When he got out of his car to help him, apparently a tremendous struggle ensued in which my father was killed. His body was stuffed in the trunk of the other car, and we never saw him again.

"Though my parents had always taken us to church on Sunday, in those early years I didn't know my Creator. Yet it didn't stop me from praying: 'God, if You are there, bring my father back to me.'

"Seven long months later, a hunter came upon the remains of my dad in a field twenty miles south of Denver. I remember thinking, *I guess there isn't a God, because*

365 Ways to Tell Your Child *"I LOVE YOU"*

(continued)

219. Encourage your son or daughter to bring friends over to visit, and talk with them to get to know them better. Be polite even to any of them you don't like.
220. On the first crisp Saturday of the fall, pass around the football together in the front yard.
221. Paint the trim on the house together.

He didn't hear my prayers. The grim reality began to sink in: My dad would never again come home to us.

"My world came apart at the seams.

"At one time my ambition was to follow in my father's footsteps and become president of the Coors Brewery, but during those shell-shocked teen years, that starry-eyed vision dissipated. Instead, when I graduated from prep school, I entered pre-law studies at Mercer University in Macon, Georgia. I majored in sorority and fraternity, rather than academics. After posting a miserable grade-point average my first year, I wound up in Marine Corps boot camp in San Diego.

"It didn't take me long to realize that being both a Coors and a Marine was going to be the most demanding challenge I had ever faced. To physically survive the rigors of being a Marine with a famous last name, I learned I would have to become physically strong and mentally tough. I took up weightlifting and the study of martial arts. My weight increased from 195 to 272 pounds — almost solid muscle.

"On the outside I was rough and tough. But each time I battled someone who tried to cross me, a confused, frustrated soul screamed out: 'Please, somebody, recognize what is really happening to me on the inside!'

"A huge void had been growing even bigger in my life, and I was hopelessly trying to fill it. I achieved the respect of my fellow Marines, but the void was still there. I took up jogging, running more two thousand miles a year — and while it did a great deal for my physique, I could not escape the nagging emptiness and anguish inside.

"Then I decided to marry my high school sweetheart, and I was sure total happiness would at last be mine. Five minutes after Betty Jane (B.J.) McCullough and I walked the aisle in the summer of 1967, I knew marriage was not the total answer.

"I returned to college, this time earning a degree from the University of Denver School of Business. After graduating I set a goal of making a million dollars by the time I was thirty. This would no doubt give me the peace of mind that had eluded me all these years, and at the same time earn respect from both relatives and friends.

"I chose the world of investments to seek my fortune, joining the Denver office of a New York brokerage firm. In addition to buying and selling stocks for my clients, I began trading commodities for my own account. I soon discovered that the commodities business is one of the fastest ways to go from riches to rags. I got deeply involved in buying up coffee contracts just before the price suddenly began to collapse. My dream of early wealth evaporated.

365 Ways to Tell Your Child ***"I LOVE YOU"***

(continued)

222. On a "rough" day for the child, let a small forgotten chore go "unnoticed."
223. As an exercise in helping you be more sensitive to your child, ask yourself, "What are the most challenging or difficult issues in my child's life? What concerns weigh heaviest upon him at this time?"

"Not long afterward I turned up at the Adolph Coors Company, asking one of my uncles for a job. I was surprised when he told me, 'No, I don't think so. But out of respect for your father, I'll direct you to the employment office down the hall. Why don't you stop in and fill out the necessary forms. We'll let you know if there's a place for you in our organization.' With my pride dashed, I left my uncle's office and proceeded down the hall to the employment office to make an application.

"Three months later, I was told to report to the brewery. Not knowing what my first job would be, I wore a coat and tie, expecting to start in middle management. Imagine my surprise when I was told my first assignment: 'Go to the Hospitality Center, Adolph. You're going to be a tour guide.' Months later I found myself scrubbing fermenting tanks.

"Some have wondered why I would be asked to work in such positions at a company my dad used to direct. For one thing, starting out as a common laborer is not unusual for future executives, especially if your last name happens to be Coors. I soon realized that having the name of Adolph Coors necessitated my learning the business from the ground up.

"Early one morning, while returning home from working the graveyard shift at the brewery, I fell asleep at the wheel of my Volkswagen convertible. While traveling at

365 Ways to Tell Your Child ***"I LOVE YOU"***

(continued)

224. Enjoy talking together about your answers to this question: "What are your biggest dreams for the future?"
225. Talk with your child about the most significant prayer requests you have — and pray for them together.
226. Join your child in his room, and build a fort with mattresses and sheets.

365 Ways to Tell Your Child **"I LOVE YOU"**

(continued)

227. Play basketball together.
228. Ask your child what special needs in his life you can pray for.
229. Have a snowball fight (let your kids cream you).
230. Serve your child breakfast in bed.

a rate of forty-five miles per hour, I hit an oncoming car. The man driving the other vehicle suffered numerous broken ribs, requiring a lengthy stay in the hospital. I slipped in and out of consciousness for six days. It took me two years to recover.

"During this time I began asking myself three questions: Adolph Coors, who are you? Why are you here on this earth? And where are you going with your life?

"Meanwhile, B.J.'s patience with my relentless search for ways of filling the cavernous void in my life was running thin. Our marriage was strained, to put it mildly. I kept insisting an answer was out there somewhere, but not even our vacation home on a beautiful mountain lake, with three boats parked by the dock, gave us any lasting joy.

"In my early years of employment at the brewery, I had met Lowell Sund, who was vice-president of administration. One night I invited him and his wife, Vera, over for dinner. As we listened intently for five solid hours, the Sunds opened their hearts to B.J. and me — including sharing with us the gospel.

"It blew me away. I wondered: *Could this be what I've been looking for all these years? Could Jesus Christ fill my void and give me a purpose for living?* I never knew that, by an act of my will, I needed to invite Christ into my life. Nor was I aware I could have a personal relationship with

231. Play dominoes, checkers, chess, or backgammon together.
232. Wash windows as a team: Together at each window, one of you clean the inside while the other does the outside. Promise yourselves something special when you're through.
233. Bring your child along when you go to assist a friend or neighbor in need.

Him, and that by knowing Jesus I could be assured that all my sins have been forgiven, and that I would spend eternity with Him in heaven.

"That night, as we were preparing for bed, B.J. and I commented to each other, 'You know, these people have what we need. They aren't even weird or strange.' In the back of my mind, however, I was considering one more option: Divorce. I decided to start with separation.

"While I lived away from my family, Lowell gave me a book that I highly recommend: *Do Yourself A Favor and Love Your Wife*, by Page Williams. It taught me that a real man is not one with bulging muscles or a 'Macho Marine' image, but one who has his priorities in line with God's priorities. That means God must be first in his life, followed by his wife, his children, and friends.

"I cried my way through the book, reading it several times. It clearly showed me how wrong I had been. One day I called B.J. and simply asked if she would give me a second chance. I told her, 'I want to be the husband you deserve and the father my four-year-old son needs.' B.J. said yes.

"During my absence, Vera Sund had already led B.J. into a personal relationship with Jesus Christ, and the profound change I observed in her led me to realize that, indeed, Jesus Christ was real. Soon I asked Christ into my heart with a simple invitation: 'Come in.'

"Total love and peace instantly flooded me. Suddenly,

all the things that I had been reading and hearing, the faith I had witnessed in my wife — it all made sense. All I could do was sit and cry, something I hadn't done since I was a little boy. All the pain and hurt that had been trapped inside of me for thirty years came rushing out with the tears.

"Before long, B.J. and I had the opportunity to share the details of our conversion with my mother. She was very interested in what had happened to both of us. Three days after talking with Mom, she had a massive stroke while vacationing with friends in Aspen. She died just a few hours later.

"For a long time I agonized over the questions of whether or not she trusted the Lord for her salvation. But after much prayer, He has given me peace that she did make a decision for Christ, and is with Him now.

"Life after salvation is like a honeymoon as you rejoice in the Lord's peace, love, and the changes He has made in your life. But part of the growing process means actively applying His principles to your life. This can be painful, but it is necessary if we are to receive all that He has for us.

"More than two years after I had asked Jesus Christ into my life, I still needed to forgive the man who killed my

365 Ways to Tell Your Child ***"I LOVE YOU"***

(continued)

234. Let your child see and hear you explaining the gospel to non-Christians. Talk together about it afterward.
235. On Halloween, instead of trick-or-treating or getting into the witches-and-goblins scene, get together as a family and cut crosses into pumpkins and set candles in them, to symbolize Christ's complete victory over death and evil.

father. Initially, I tried to avoid the issue, but through the persistence of a friend, who regularly visited the Colorado State Penitentiary, I finally agreed to go. My friend called the warden the night before our trip and asked him to arrange a meeting for me with my father's killer.

"When we arrived, however, the warden told us that the prisoner had rejected our request. Not knowing what to do, at first I hesitated. Then I asked the warden for some paper. Sitting down I wrote a note to the man that read in part, 'I ask for your forgiveness for the hatred I've had for you for seventeen years, and I forgive you for what you did to me and my family.'

"I could have never worked through this problem by myself. I was just being obedient to what God was telling me to do in His word: 'Forgive, and it will be forgiven you.' On my own I didn't have the ability to forgive as He asked me to, but through my willingness to completely follow Him, He gave me the strength to write that short letter.

"On my way out through the prison gates, I remarked to my friend, 'I don't have the hatred anymore.' He looked at me and replied, 'Well, when you're obedient, God will remove negative things from your life.'

"Twice more I visited the prison, hoping to visit my father's murderer. Each time he refused to talk with me. On my last trip, though, an inmate approached me and related what had happened as a result of my note. 'He got the note and it had an impact on him,' he told me. Then

*365 Ways to Tell Your Child **"I LOVE YOU"***

(continued)

236. Go through old boxes in the attic together.
237. To think about: When you consider the biblical command to "love the LORD your God with all your heart," what relevance could it have for the way you love your child?
238. Don't be afraid to admit to your child when you're wrong.
239. Go swimming together.

365 Ways to Tell Your Child **"I LOVE YOU"**

(continued)

240. When the weather turns stormy, sit together at a picture window and watch it in wonder.
241. Tell your child how you most want to improve in life in the coming year, and ask him to pray for you.
242. Discuss together this question: "If you could design and build your own mansion, what would it be like?"

he added: 'You might be interested in knowing that your letter has gone from cell to cell throughout this entire prison. You'll never have any idea of the impact this had on the prisoners here, Mr. Coors.'

"A few years ago, the man who killed my father was paroled. We have never communicated, but even if I never get to talk with him, I still pray that he will experience firsthand the REALITY of God's forgiveness.

"For me, applying the principles of forgiveness didn't stop at the Colorado State Penitentiary. Forgiveness is to be practiced daily, and has extended to many areas of my life, particularly to family and business relationships.

"As you may have guessed, I didn't exactly fit the family mold, and I had many problems with various family members who disliked my proud attempts to carve my own path. As strange as it may sound, reaching forgiveness in a well-known and highly successful family such as mine can be more difficult than coming to grips with the loss of a loved one. But I trust that many of my relatives truly understand that God has called me to a different task.

"Last year, I visited one of my uncles in his office at the brewery. During the hour we had together, I shared with him the same thing the Lord has asked me to communicate to business and government leaders throughout this country. As I was leaving, I turned to him and said, 'I have

365 Ways to Tell Your Child *"I LOVE YOU"*

(continued)

243. Look at old photograph albums together.
244. Think about what you would like your life to be like at age forty, age fifty, age sixty, and age seventy. Then talk about your dreams and desires with your child.
245. Give your child something you like (your favorite sweatshirt, your dessert at dinner tonight).

never mentioned this to you before, but I want to take this opportunity to tell you I love you.'

"I now support my family through investments management and speaking engagements. Over the past nine years since my departure from the brewery, I have endured a tough education in business. When you possess a well-known name it seems to attract plenty of people who, it seems, lie awake at night inventing ways to exploit you. The sad truth in my experience is that many of these people have been professing Christians. But in such cases, I have learned to remember Jesus' admonition to forgive 'seventy times seven.'

"These experiences have also taught me that no matter how painful the losses, I can't keep my sights on money. There is something much more important at stake — reaching a deeper understanding of God's love, and how He hates the sin but loves the sinner.

"As I fully grasp what Christ did for me on the Cross of Calvary, I realize that I have no right to hate anybody — not even the man who killed my father."

(As told to *Voice*, and used by permission)

PART THREE

EMBRACE THE WIND

CHASE OR EMBRACE?

I HAD JOINED thirteen undercover narcotics agents who were monitoring (and sweating out) a multi-thousand-dollar drug deal involving a frightened "snitch" — he had agreed to set up his drug buddies in exchange for a reduction in his penalty (and a little heroin on the side). It wasn't my idea of an enjoyable Saturday night, but it was the only way at the moment to spend time with a great undercover cop who also happened to be my brother.

A "snitch," I learned, will do anything for a fix. Any kid thinking about smoking a joint should see an addict craving a syringe-full of heroin, like a deer panting for water after being chased by a pack of dogs on a hot summer day.

Sad thing about heroin — there is never a lasting high; the fix is only artificial, temporary. Then the user has to steal, deal, or con to get another one.

Getting an ego trip from someone telling us we're beautiful or impressive can be a lot like a drug fix. The words sound encouraging at the time, but the high never lasts. You always want more.

Solomon called it "chasing the wind."

Some of the most insecure girls I know are beautiful. Many of the most insecure young guys I know are great athletes. Their phone rings often with praise for their external gift. But their heart hasn't had a date in years.

Glamor girls in malls and in front of mirrors are chasing the wind with makeup brushes.

Star athletes chase the wind while looking for their latest write-up in the sports pages.

Weightlifters go to beaches wearing brief swimsuits and greased bodies — and they chase the wind.

My big, black dog *waits* on our front porch for me to come home, just to have his ears scratched — oh, how

365 Ways to Tell Your Child "I LOVE YOU"

(continued)

246. Go horseback-riding together.
247. Laugh together.
248. Cry together.
249. "Bury" a treasure somewhere in your house or yard, put together a map and some cryptic clues, and help your kids conduct a treasure hunt.

good that feels. But after I walk away, his ears will itch again...and more so! "Scratch my ears!"

Chasing the wind...ever tried it?

The merry-go-round spins faster and faster. *Here's my ego...quick, feed it!*

I *feel* for people like that. As I grew up, I thought I must have been one of the most insecure people alive. In my younger years I longed to be chosen for the little league baseball team. Later I would have given anything if a girl would have noticed me, or if a guy had called and asked me to go play football. In college, when accolades came, I couldn't get enough!

It took a giant tragedy in my life, and lots of smaller ones, to wake me up to the encouraging voice of God.

Then I discovered: Hey, this is no quick fix.

Don't chase the wind — embrace it!

EMBRACE THE WIND

IN FRONT OF THE JEERING WORLD, Jesus gasped for air, all His weight bearing down on the few points where His nailed flesh pressed the wood. He stretched His arms open for us as far as He could, as if saying, "I'll hang here till dark, if that's what it takes to let you know YOU'RE WORTH DYING FOR." He didn't just say cheaply, "I forgive you," but He absorbed the eternal damage I've caused. He became a curse to reinstate my perfection and my place in

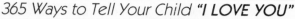

365 Ways to Tell Your Child "I LOVE YOU"

(continued)

250. Climb a tree together.
251. Treat your child like a fishing line: Give some slack, but don't let him run away or get tangled up.
252. To think about: When you consider the biblical command to "love the LORD your God with all your soul," what relevance could it have for the way you love your child?

God's flawless kingdom. That's a fact I need to accept every day. That is my net worth.

One night as we talked tenderly of the Cross, my ten-year-old daughter cried out, "Dad, did God take away the pain?"

"No, Sweetheart. Jesus felt all of the pain. All of it."

All of it.

Last night that same sensitive-hearted daughter found a roll of brown paper and tore off three 4-foot-long strips, and made posters in beautiful ten-year-old art. She hung one in our room, one in her sister's room, and one in her brothers' room. Each one said, "Thanks for being the best in the world. I love you so much." It didn't fit the latest home decor schemes in *Better Homes & Gardens*, but we'll let those posters hang around for a long, long time.

It's good to hear the same thing from God: "I love you so much."

Swallowing that eternal time-released vitamin is the great make-over that every woman's magazine is seeking to find for aging faces and egos.

Coming to grips with God's view of me through Christ-colored glasses reminds me of my Dad watching me play in a college football game against Ohio State. The game attendance was 75,000, but as far as I was concerned, the only loyal, cheering fan who mattered was my Daddy.

Listen to a powerful passage: "This is the mystery which has been hidden from the past ages and generations but has now been manifested...it is *Christ in you*, the hope of glory!" (Colossians 1:26-27).

That's the encouragement of encouragements.

That's the hope of all hopes.

Please: If necessary, gently remove any denominational barriers that may be holding you back from Christ, and let Him in. It's the end of empty religion and futile reaching for God.

It's God's personal walk with you!

It's His letter in the envelope of your heart.

Let me urge you to make a brilliant discovery, with eyes as fresh as the April breeze that blows new life into these Ozark Mountains from whence I write.

Discover my friend *Jesus*, the tiny baby born amid decaying straw and cow manure to a half-amazed teenage girl.

He was human, like us. The little boy with dirt under His fingernails. The teenager with zits who had to blow His nose when He cried. The young carpenter who bent a nail, and whose thumbnail turned black after He hit it with a hammer.

Jesus — so human that He got goose bumps after going swimming... yet so divine that He could say "Father, forgive them" as He died the most painful death ever devised by man. (This was in a time when crosses weren't jewelry, but rugged, splintered trees to die on.) Then He bought eternal paradise for the millions who would

365 Ways to Tell Your Child ***"I LOVE YOU"***

(continued)

253. Allow your child to make some mistakes; when he does, instead of condemning him, work together toward a solution.
254. As you think about your way of life and the example you provide for your children, ask God to empower you to live out the gospel of Christ (the greatest love of all).

become like a little child and trust Him like a special Daddy.

Jesus — the man so misunderstood that His hometown buddies tried to push Him off a cliff... yet so well understood by a cheating tax collector (who got caught out on a limb) that to the people he had defrauded he gave back four times as much as he had taken.

Jesus — so fragile in His infancy that He had to be taken to a foreign country to escape being killed by a crazy king's sword... yet so powerful today that the entire universe shudders as it awaits His final shout.

Jesus — so powerful and majestic that the expanses of creation came from the snap of His finger... yet so personal, so knowable, so approachable that He could slip His fingers between yours and grip your fleshy palm with His nail-printed hands.

Is He a Clark Kent/Superman? No, He is much more human than Clark Kent and infinitely more divine than Superman. Clark Kent knew a passionate "I love you" for an attractive female newspaper reporter. Jesus said, "I don't condemn you" to a half-clothed adulteress who stood trembling on a deathbed of stones. Superman flies at the speed of light. Jesus invented light. He *is* light.

In appearance, is He some Tom Cruz, Clint Eastwood, or Robert Redford — but with a halo and wings?

Hardly. Isaiah implies that He was quite common in appearance. Yet billions have followed Him and clung to His presence; they have followed Him not into a theater of

365 Ways to Tell Your Child ***"I LOVE YOU"***

(continued)

255. Remind your child often that he is created in God's image.
256. Worship together at church *and* at home.
257. Celebrate your child's achievements and victories, but don't let him feel he has to "win" in order to be loved. Accept and love him at all times, and communicate that your greatest joy is because of *who he is,* not what he does.

365 Ways to Tell Your Child *"I LOVE YOU"*

(continued)

258. Tell your child, "You contribute so much to this family."
259. Ask your child to tell you about any special prayer requests and needs for his friends, and then pray together for them.
260. Tell your child, "You have many special friends who think you're wonderful."
261. Tell your child, "You're the apple of my eye."

make-believe and entertainment, but into the arena of eternity.

Do you know this Jesus?

Do you really know Him as if He were a faithful father, affirming mother, tender child, and a loyal, lifelong spouse, all in one package?

He *is* that loving and lovable...and more.

Perhaps you're shy about this kind of love because way down deep something tells you that to love Him means you must honor Him 86,400 seconds every day. It means that the 63,700,000 thoughts you think every year should *all* be His. It means you'll be called to fight like a faithful soldier to keep every letter and stroke of His commandments.

To love Him, you know, is to proclaim Him, like a Paul Revere on horseback urgently stampeding his message in the dark: *"Jesus is coming! Jesus is coming!* Prepare your heart, prepare your home! *Jesus is coming!"*

He *deserves* this kind of love — and then some. Give it to Him and you'll find yourself swept away by a tornado of exciting, happy, tearful, unpredictable experiences — a new existence in which the nerve impulses in your fingers will touch the eternal, a refreshing new atmosphere to inhale with every remaining breath you take in this ever-so-brief moment on planet Earth.

Think — Think —

Jesus — that's Him!

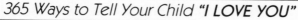

262. With toy building blocks, work together to make the highest object you can.
263. When your child feels like a failure, reassure him by saying, "I believe in you; I know you can do better next time."
264. When you must punish, give an explanation: "I had to punish you this way because I care for you and want the best for you."

FEELING LIKE A '10'

IF YOU WANT TO SEE the mystery unfold and bloom, then realize that the secret is not just in the big makeover. It's in the routine makeup we apply day after day.

In Philippians 3, Paul quietly wrote the most encouraging verse, I believe, in the Bible: "However, let us keep living by the same standard to which we have attained."

To God you are a "10." That's done. It's complete. You're perfect, forgiven, wonderful, God's prize, His child!

Now, to feel all of those great things...live by them! Live as if you *know* they're true — because you do know they're true.

Listen to the One who made you. Get away from the mirrors that tell you you're only a "9" or a "7" or a "4" or worse. Maybe glamor magazines mirror a "5" to you: "Be more slender, be more in-style, wear more expensive makeup." TV mirrors a "3" to you: "Live a little, loosen up; you gotta be more hip, take a pill, have a sip." Your bathroom mirror (if you take it seriously) tells you you're a "2" this morning: "Those wrinkles, those gray hairs, those balding spots, those extra pounds."

Worst of all, an uncleansed conscience tells you you're a "1" — you've blown it...it's too late...nobody can help you now. Sorry.

You're feeling burned. And every time you let the sin happen, you throw gasoline on the fire.

Ready for a make-over?

Give Christ charge of your life. Go to the mountain top with the One who died to set you free, and who lives to fill your sail.

Embrace the wind.

Then...you're ready to give it away.

So get on your knees and...and let it start now.

GOD'S TEARS

AT SUPPER TONIGHT the phone rang. The unfamiliar but desperate voice of a mom pleaded with me to go to the local hospital, where her daughter had been rushed after taking forty-two sleeping pills in an effort to say a permanent goodbye. I went — and it was an evening I'll never forget.

Kim really didn't want to die. She just felt so alone, and didn't have the energy to face another day. "Kim," I said, "if you could have anything you want, what would it be?"

A smile sneaked across her face. "I'd like to have Jesus in my heart. I want to know He's there."

Using God's wonderful and assuring words — "Behold I stand at the door and knock. If anyone hears my voice

365 Ways to Tell Your Child "I LOVE YOU"

(continued)

265. To think about: When you consider the biblical command to "love the LORD your God with all your mind," what relevance could it have for the way you love your child?
266. On a day when the weather is adverse, offer to help your child with his paper route.
267. Make popcorn balls together.

and opens the door..." — I rolled out the red carpet to the door of her heart.

As she asked Jesus in, she wept many tears of sheer relief.

"Kim," I queried, "what are those tears?"

She looked at me steadily, half smiling, half shaking, half sobbing. "I don't know, but I think they're God."

That's exactly what they were.

REMEMBER THE MYSTERY

AFTER SPEAKING to a thousand enthusiastic teenagers at "Girls' State" last summer, a beautiful, brown-eyed brunette came up to me with mascara streaks running down her powdered cheeks. As she clutched her boyfriend's senior ring which dangled clumsily on her finger, she cried softly, "I feel so guilty — we've...you see we had sex and I got pregnant, and, well, I made the worst mistake of my life; I had an abortion." Her tears flowed like rain.

I began to counsel. "How long ago did it happen?"

"About six months ago. It was so awful. I'm so awful." The tears increased.

I looked steadily into her bloodshot eyes. "Sandy, are you still sleeping with him?"

She looked surprised. "Yes — how'd you know?"

365 Ways to Tell Your Child "I LOVE YOU"

(continued)

268. With sticks or straws, string, and paper cutouts, make mobiles together.
269. With your child, take turns answering this question: "What is the funniest thing that ever happened to you?"
270. Allow your son or daughter to go to work with you and be your helper.

365 Ways to Tell Your Child "*I LOVE YOU*"

(continued)

271. After punishing your child for striking a match in an unsafe place, take him to a safe place and together light a whole box of matches.
272. Help your child with a school project. Encourage creativity.
273. Put up a tire swing in the tallest tree around, and swing together.

"Princess, your guilt is not so much for what you *did.* God can handle past sin. That's His specialty. It's what you are *doing* that hurts you so much."

It's true for young Sandy...it's true for me...it's true for you: Feeling good about yourself comes from living in God's purity. *Today.*

You *know* God's amazing love when you *live* in God's amazing love.

When He says, "Blessed are the pure in heart for they shall see God," he means you'll see God in the twinkle of your own eyes when you look in the mirror. You'll also see God as you hug your child, as you hold your spouse's hand, as you marvel at a sunset or see a tiny butterfly float majestically through the air. You'll feel God's tender arms wrap around your emotions as you thank Him confidently for His forgiving power. You'll weep tears of deep happiness as you sing those familiar hymns and praise choruses.

A pure heart that longs to please your Lord is fertile soil for planting the seed of God's most encouraging words.

A pure heart is a heart controlled by God's touch, a touch that comes through your ears, your eyes, your nose, your mouth, and your fingers. Is it God who is touching your heart when you select a movie? A TV show? A radio station? A relationship?

Hard? You bet it's hard. In fact it's impossible.

Except... except... remember the mystery: "Christ in you." My Bible says, "I can do all things through Christ who strengthens me."

I can't think of a greater challenge on this earth than to be an example of purity to your kids. When you're serious about it, they're serious about it.

God plants seeds in families like that!

I've discovered that teenagers (and all kids) feel best about themselves when they make the right decisions. They feel worse about themselves when they sin. Are you allowing your kids to get into bad decision-making habits? Or are you giving them good guidance and opportunities to develop their decision-making ability? And can they see good decision-making modeled daily in *you?*

INFILTRATION

KATHY FIRST CAME to our youth group at age sixteen, shortly after her alcoholic father shot himself. She was angry as a Texas rattlesnake. We talked often and hammered through walls of bitterness. I fed her God's Word.

After this sweet-spirited, baby-faced, brown-eyed girl left high school, she began smoking pot regularly. Then, as is so often the case, she did speed, acid, and anything else she could afford. With only a waitress's salary to

365 Ways to Tell Your Child **"I LOVE YOU"**

(continued)

274. Play marbles together.
275. For fun on the family room floor: Imitate animals together.
276. Find extra work projects your child can do to earn money.
277. Make a bug collection together (or work together on any collection — baseball cards, dolls, old coins, etc.).

365 Ways to Tell Your Child *"I LOVE YOU"*

(continued)

278. To think about: When you consider the biblical command to "love the LORD your God with all your strength," what relevance could it have for the way you love your child?
279. Invite your child's friends over, build a mountain on a tray out of ice cream scoops and whipped cream (with all the toppings), and then eat it.

support a growing habit, she began to mainline "T's & Blues," a type of poor man's heroin.

Soon she was dying. Though only in her twenties, her vital organs had begun to fail, like those of an eighty-year-old. Bruises from hundreds of needle invasions crawled up and down her arms and legs, like patterns on a patchwork quilt.

We continued to stay in touch.

Three days ago this letter came to my mailbox. I'm still celebrating!

> Dear Joe,
>
> Jesus is the reason for the season. Do you remember, Joe, when you told me a long time ago that every day you would say a prayer for me? I believe in my heart that you did that, because ten years later it was answered. Our prayers were answered! Joe, this is Kathy, and my husband and I asked Jesus into our lives. And every day we ask God to let us live every minute as a Christian. We started reading the Bible together and joined a church and a Bible study and began to grow like caterpillars. Joe, the feeling of sharing Christ with someone you love and someone you spend your life with is the same feeling I felt when you and I prayed many years ago. So as my husband and I were getting our house Christlike I found this book my friend had given me and I had laid aside and

365 Ways to Tell Your Child *"I LOVE YOU"*

(continued)

280. Make a wildflower collection together.
281. If your child breaks something, help him fix it.
282. When you're enjoying being and talking together, ask your child, "What have been the toughest and most discouraging things you've ever had to work through and overcome?"
283. Have a game night together.

forgotten. I read it and my husband and I read it together. Parts made us cry — like, if I were the only person, Christ would have died for me.

Well, I've been through a lot, but only because I was following Satan — how I let him run my heart. And God waited for me. And now I have made peace with my Lord, and when temptation comes around I let God handle it.

I want to learn everything I missed about Christ. I want to be the best Christian I can be. I want you and Debbie Jo to know that flowers grew from our youth group. Everything you ever taught me is in my mind. Joe, you were my best friend.

I'm sorry for my past life — to you, to God, to myself. Please forgive me for all the things I've done to you in the past. But when your mind is run by drugs, drugs, and more drugs, you don't care who you hurt — even God!

In Christ, Kathy

Kathy could not escape the infiltration of God's Word that we had "mainlined" into her heart more than a dozen years ago. Thousands of injections of drugs couldn't drown it out. Millions of rebellious thoughts couldn't quench it.

"God's Word does not come back void" (Isaiah 55:11).

And it's the most encouraging message ever written.

HABIT OF THE HEART

AS I SPEAK TO TEENS across the country I often ask them, "How many of you memorize Scripture with your parents at home?" What percentage of them do you think answer Yes? Fifty? Twenty-five? Ten? Five?

Try less than two percent. I almost fall over every time I receive the same small answer.

In Psalms 1, God promises us that our kids will be *blessed* (prosperous, fruitful, persevering in tough times) if they will meditate on God's Word day and night, and not dwell on bad advice from peers, TV, rock music, movies, and so on.

He *promises* us! So why don't we help them do it?

Can you see why we're losing so many in this generation of kids?

Several years ago I sat near the sidelines on a basketball court in Oxford, Mississippi, admiring my two camp director cohorts and their basketball skills that had outlived their colorful college careers.

While they played, I was (believe it or not) pecking away at my Scripture memory work (I have to stay at it as often as possible to get those words into my head, with its thickness like a burglar-proof vault). A giant black man sat down beside me, and we began a casual conversation

365 Ways to Tell Your Child **"I LOVE YOU"**

(continued)

284. In a moment when you and your child are relaxed and enjoying each other's company, tell your child about your spiritual past — your wonderings and wanderings, how you found Christ, and how Christ changed your life.
285. Have an "open forum" sharing time at dinner, and let your children express themselves fully.

as the game raged on a few feet away. Johnny played basketball for Ole Miss. He was a bone-crusher — one of the best-looking athletes this old college coach ever laid eyes on. In a few minutes our conversation landed squarely on Johnny's relationship with the Lord. After many difficult teenage years, Johnny was now ready for a major overhaul in his life. At ten o'clock that night, Johnny Boatman became a new man in Christ.

He kept growing in spite of the adverse peer pressure constantly surrounding him on the Ole Miss campus. A year after he gave his heart to Christ, I asked him what force inside him gave him the energy to say no to the drinking and sex flowing so freely around him.

Johnny smiled a smile that would have melted a tyrannical dictator's heart. "It was my grandmom," he began, reflecting happily on his childhood. "When I was a young kid she would memorize Scripture with me for hours. Those verses never left me!"

Today I visited at length with an ex-drug-addict kid from a wealthy suburb. He had begun taking and dealing drugs at age thirteen. At age eighteen he stopped cold, and hasn't touched a drug since. He's now twenty-two, and has graduated from college.

He sounded so good today, so in control, so full of hope.

"Will," I asked him with wonder, "what has kept you clean in the last four and a half years?"

365 Ways to Tell Your Child ***"I LOVE YOU"***

(continued)

286. Plan a day each month that is your child's special day: Do the things he enjoys.
287. Have your child help with your daily activities at home — cooking and baking, cleaning, mowing, repairing, etc. Use this time as a teaching process. Don't just assign tasks; help your child accomplish them.

365 Ways to Tell Your Child *"I LOVE YOU"*

(continued)

288. Be consistent in your discipline. Establish guidelines and follow through with what you say you'll do.
289. In love, challenge your child to make goals (challenge him to stretch himself) and to strive for them (press on!).
290. Always take photographs on your child's special occasions.
291. Take your child out for ice cream after school.

In telling his story, Will went as straight to the meat as a hungry tiger: "When I was doing drugs my heart was softer than the other druggies'. They were having fun on their way to hell — I wasn't. I was scared because God was always in the back of my mind. My folks grew me up feeding me God's Word, and the only reason I quit drugs was because of my relationship with Christ. God's Word pierced my thoughts. My friends were ignorant; they didn't care. I always knew God cared and He was waiting for me; He didn't hate my guts.

"My parents loved me unconditionally while they hated what I was doing. I'm the prodigal son. I'm just glad my parents taught me how to come home!"

Here's the formula (it works better than Gerber's on a baby, and is more incredible than Ralph Lauren with a teen):

- *You* (especially Dad!) get excited about God's Word. When your kids invade your quiet time a few times, they get the idea you live with your nose in God's Word.
- Memorize Scripture consistently. Your kids will admire and desire your tenacity.
- Memorize Scripture a chapter at a time. Memorizing only individual verses can keep you from the deeper meaning, emotion, and drama that come from

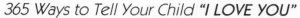

365 Ways to Tell Your Child *"I LOVE YOU"*

(continued)

292. Compliment your children for their truly distinctive qualities. Let each child know that he is unique, and make him feel special for who he is.
293. Walk the dog together.
294. Cook breakfast together on Saturday morning.
295. Help your child wash his bike (or tricycle).

understanding the context. When you memorize chapters in Paul's letter to the Philippians, you feel as if you are right there with him in that Roman jail. It's amazing!

- Feed the Word to your kids tonight by starting a memory passage together. (Age three is a good time to start; age ninety isn't too late to begin.)

Here's a sample listing of verses and passages to memorize, broken down according to the child's age:

Age 3

Psalm 23

Age 4

Psalm 1	Matthew 5:16
John 3:16	John 10:10
1 John 1:9	Revelation 3:20

The Lord's Prayer
(Matthew 6:9-13)

Age 5

Romans 3:23	1 Corinthians 13
Galatians 5:22-23	Philippians 2:3-5
Colossians 3:23	1 Peter 2:2

Age 6

Psalm 100	Matthew 5:1-16
John 1:12	Romans 5:8
2 Corinthians 12:9	Ephesians 6:1-3

Age 7

Luke 2:1-20	John 14:1-4
Romans 6:23	Romans 8:1
Romans 12:1-3	2 Timothy 3:16-17

Ages 8-9

Psalm 103	John 14:5-11
Acts 1:8	Philippians 2

Ages 10-11

John 1:1-14	Philippians 3:13-14
John 14:12-21	Philippians 4

1 Thessalonians 5:16-18

(And so on. One to two chapters per year is not too much.)

- Do it enthusiastically. Be contagious in your own excitement for Scripture memory.

365 Ways to Tell Your Child ***"I LOVE YOU"***

(continued)

296. Ask your child, "What have been the most encouraging things that ever happened to you — things that really helped you grow in confidence?"
297. As you think about your responsibility in raising your children wisely, ask God to empower you to "bring them up in the training and instruction of the Lord" (Ephesians 6:4).

- Chip away at it patiently, daily.
- Apply God's Word to your life, and help your kids apply it to their lives throughout the day.
- Center your family devotionals around the verses you're learning. Have the kids take turns leading these devotional times.

  (In the back of this book is a month's supply of encouraging, hope-building family devotionals. (They were written by my family and co-workers, my teenage camp friends, and me.) Share these with your family in the next thirty days. I hope they'll help God's Word become a habit of the heart for every member of your family.

DAILY BREAD

THE MORE YOU MEMORIZE and meditate on Scripture, the more meaningful it is, and the more meaningful it is, the easier it is to memorize and think about it. It's a wonderful cycle.

Jamie Jo memorized the Lord's Prayer a long time ago. On the following pages are some of her thoughts about this passage, which I've helped her put into writing as a way to encourage other kids. I hope you see in her words not only the rich reward of meditating on Scripture, but also the priceless principles of finding the basis for self-esteem in a secure relationship with God.

365 Ways to Tell Your Child ***"I LOVE YOU"***

(continued)

298. Build a snowman together.
299. Volunteer to help with your son's or daughter's youth group at church.
300. Say something encouraging about your child in front of his friends.
301. Mow the lawn occasionally when it's your child's turn.

365 Ways to Tell Your Child *"I LOVE YOU"*

(continued)

302. Sit outside some night and talk together as you watch the moon and stars.
303. Talk about your favorite hymns, and why you like them.
304. Go all out to celebrate your son's or daughter's birthday.
305. Make up a secret code language, and write messages to one another.

"Our Father..."

"The most important thing that ever happened to me was when I asked Jesus into my heart. I can still remember (even though it has been almost six years ago now) the pajamas I was wearing the night it happened (they were yellow with red stripes, a white stripe, and footies). That was a night I'll never forget.

"When Jesus came into my heart, God became my Father — *my* Father! Sure, He was Jesus' Dad too, but He is mine just as much. Since that night I've learned how much God really loves *me*. I've also learned that He even has a plan for my life.

"I know how much God loves me because I can feel how much my Daddy loves me. He tells me he loves me often and takes me places. He does nice things for me, and every time I'm hurt and my heart breaks, he ties it back together again.

"That's the way God is, but I think since His heart is bigger than my Dad's or anyone else's on earth, His love must be greater.

"The first Bible verse I learned (when I was three) was John 3:16 — 'For God so loved the world that He gave His only Son, so that whoever believes in Him will not perish but have everlasting life.' That's a lot of love. It's really great to think He'd even let His Son die on the cross for me, so that when I die I won't have to go to a place of darkness but will spend eternity with God in heaven.

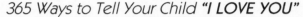

365 Ways to Tell Your Child *"I LOVE YOU"*

(continued)

306. Put child's school pictures up on the refrigerator.
307. Make a photo gallery somewhere in your home, and display your children's school pictures from each year.
308. Go jogging together.
309. Take binoculars and go bird-watching together.

"So now I can be very happy knowing I don't need to be afraid, because God won't let me down. When you're feeling like your life has just slipped down a slide, He picks you back up again.

"The second verse I ever learned was John 1:12. It says, 'But to as many as received Him, to them He gave the right to be a child of God.' It's a happy feeling to know I'm His little girl and He's my Dad. I want to love Him more every day."

"who art in heaven..."

"Heaven is a home that you can go to when you die after you've asked Jesus into your heart. The moment you leave this earth, you'll wake up in heaven, a place that Jesus has prepared especially for you.

"When I was six years old I learned a very special thing that Jesus told His disciples the night before He went to die on the cross. He said, 'Let not your heart be troubled. Believe in God, believe also in Me. In My Father's house are many mansions. If it were not so, I would have told you, for I go to prepare a place for you.' Heaven is a good place that God has ready for you. Even if you sin, it's still your home because Jesus paid for that sin. Your home in heaven must be a big house. It must be a nice house, a very pretty house. Only the rich live in a mansion on earth. But God doesn't care if you're rich or poor — Jesus makes you rich in God's eyes.

"I remember being the flower girl at the wedding of my babysitter, Sara. She was very pretty at that wedding and very happy. She didn't want to give up her husband for anything. She was wearing a pretty white dress trimmed with tiny pearls. This was really a special occasion! To recall Sara walking down the aisle in her bright white dress reminds me of the way the Holy Spirit brightens you up after He's inside your heart. If you get dirt on your pure heart, the dirt is like sin, and I know Christ cleanses that sin away and makes your heart pure white again. The purity gives a bride a happy life with her husband and her kids, so heaven's purity must make it a real special place.

"It's great to know my Mom and Dad and brothers and sister will be there too, because they have Jesus in their hearts just like I do. It really makes me happy knowing that we'll all have a wedding with Christ someday, and we'll never be apart."

"hallowed be Thy name..."

"When I first learned this part of the Lord's Prayer, I thought it said 'Halloween.' But it's sure not Halloween. *Hallowed* means to me that God is really big, and we should praise Him. It also means that God is holy — He is perfect.

"Last spring my Dad and I were snorkeling in the Caribbean Sea, looking for pretty fish around the coral reefs. Just outside the calm bay were big waves and a

365 Ways to Tell Your Child **"I LOVE YOU"**

(continued)

310. Play hide-n-seek with the kids (don't find them too quickly).
311. Take a day off from work and spend the whole day doing things he enjoys.
312. Ask your child, "What encouraging comments from others have been most meaningful to you?"
313. Take your child and some of his friends out for a pizza.

dangerous undertow. We decided to go just past the warning rope to see this unusual coral reef with thousands of colorful fish swimming around it. We got caught in the current and I thought we were going to drown. I was praying harder than I ever have before for God to save me. The undertow was stronger than Daddy, but it wasn't stronger than God. A big wave suddenly hit our backs and pushed us back to the rope. All I could think about was how thankful I was to be a Christian, and able to experience how big and holy and perfect God is. I praised God for saving me from drowning.

"Every night I praise God for a beautiful day for me to enjoy. Even if it is raining, I praise Him. Every day is beautiful because God supplies my needs that day. He loves me all day long, just like I feel my Mom and Dad's love all day long."

"Thy kingdom come..."

"A kingdom is a special place for a king to be. When I was smaller, we had a hideout that we called our 'kingdom.' We'd go up there and play like kings and queens. God must be the King of everything because He made everything. This part of the prayer is a personal invitation for you and me to join Him in His kingdom.

"God's kingdom is being prepared for me and my family. Heaven must be like a kingdom. It will have gold streets with many palaces lining the sidewalks. When

365 Ways to Tell Your Child ***"I LOVE YOU"***

(continued)

314. Talk with your child about what you're learning personally about Jesus Christ.
315. On occasion, allow your son to use your credit card for a dinner date.
316. If your child has a car, help him wash it.
317. Do exercises together — jumping jacks, push-ups, sit-ups.

318. Help your child learn his spelling words or multiplication tables. Make it a game.
319. Make a tire swing for the biggest tree in your yard, and swing together on it.
320. Take your child with you on a business trip.
321. Go to the state or county fair together.

Jesus lives in someone's heart He actually engraves your name on the door of your personal palace up there. His kingdom must be a very nice place to live."

"Thy will be done..."

"You should do on earth what you'd do in heaven. God wants you to be free from sin and to always act like a Christian. To pray 'Thy will be done' is to pray, 'I give you my will, God; whatever you ask me to do, I want to do it.'

"God's will for us is found in the Bible. You can't know His plan for you if you let His Bible sit on the bookshelf and gather dust. When I read it and memorize verses from it, I learn what God's will is for me.

"The best time of the day for my Daddy and me to memorize Scripture is at night before I go to sleep. When he comes in to tell me goodnight, we memorize a new Bible verse together and talk about what it means. The next morning my brothers and my sister and Mom and Dad and I sit on their king-sized bed and we have a family devotional. Each day we take turns being the leader. It's super great to learn so much about God's will as a family.

"It is God's will for us to love each other just as Christ loved us when He was on earth, and just as He would love us if He were here in person today. When someone dies, he leaves a 'will' that tells what to do with his possessions. You have to follow that will and do exactly as he said, even

(continued)

322. Stay up as a family till past midnight on New Year's' Eve, playing games, performing skits, singing songs, and just being zany.
323. Start praying now for the spouse your son or daughter will have someday. Pray that their marriage will be strong and Christ-centered.

though he's not with you anymore. The Bible is like the 'will' Christ left us when He left this earth.

It is important for us to know God's will so you can go to heaven and take others with you. Following God's will also allows you to live a truly happy life while you're here on the earth!"

"on earth as it is heaven..."

"There will be a big war here someday, and when it's over Christ will come back with all of His children, and the earth will be without sin. There will never be another fight or argument. It will be pretty perfect. We won't have to worry because everyone will act like Christians. Jesus will be the King, and His kingdom will be lit up constantly by God's presence. There will be no need for any sun or lamp, because God will illuminate the new earth.

"There will be gates of pearls but they'll never need to be shut, because God will be our protection.

"In heaven you'll never have to be scared, and you'll never have to run to anybody or hide under your covers for protection. Once at summer camp I was scared to swing off on the trapeze above the swimming pool. My counselor was there to hold me and comfort me. She helped me get on the trapeze, and now I'm not scared of that anymore. That's the type of protection God will always give us in heaven.

"Heaven is also a place where you never have to hurt or cry again. Last year my uncle died, and I cried a lot. It will be good to see my uncle again in heaven. In heaven we'll never be sad.

"When our family was at Disney World when I was six, I lost a stuffed animal that my Dad had given me three years before. This little dog was my favorite. I was sad at first, but later it was like heaven was already here because everyone was comforting me, taking the sadness away."

"Give us this day our daily bread..."

"This phrase reminds me of our family joining hands around the table, thanking God for the food we get to eat. Our attitude is serious. You've got to really mean your prayers, or they're nothing but words.

"God is doing a great job of supplying our needs; there are a lot of things I want and don't really need, but the things I truly need He gives me. It is so good to wake up early in the morning knowing that cereal and milk will be on the table. God wants to feed me so I can go out and tell other people about Him.

"God not only provides my food each day, but He's there to meet all my needs. One of my needs each day is to have my sins forgiven. Each night when I ask Him (and really mean it) to forgive me for the mistakes I made that day, I know that He forgives me.

365 Ways to Tell Your Child ***"I LOVE YOU"***

(continued)

324. Ask your child, "If you were stranded alone on an island for a year, what would you like most to have with you, besides adequate food, water, and clothing?
325. Drive the speed limit.
326. Fasten your seat belt when you're in the car, and insist that your children do, too.

"Two years ago I realized that a lot of children in the world aren't as fortunate as I am. I saw the starving Ethiopian children on TV, and it really made me thankful for the food God provides me. It also taught me to love Him and thank Him now.

"We can help God provide those poor kids with daily bread by sending them food and Bibles. At our home we "miss a meal" and send them the money. At Sunday school our class gathers eighteen dollars a month to help feed a child. Now I take twenty-five cents of every dollar I earn or get for allowance, and put that much into a separate cup in my closet to send to those hungry children. It will make them feel good, and it makes me feel good, too."

"and forgive us our trespasses (or 'debts')..."

"Committing a trespass or having this kind of debt is like going somewhere and getting off the road. You do something you shouldn't do, such as disobeying your parents or being mean to your brother or sister, or talking back to your mom. That is a trespass, and God forgives them when we confess them to Him and ask for His forgiveness.

"A few years ago I memorized 1 John 1:9 — 'If we confess our sins, He is faithful and just to forgive us our sins, and to cleanse us from all unrighteousness.' It's sort of like He writes down all our bad marks on a chalkboard, then erases it clean when you go to Him and ask for forgiveness.

365 Ways to Tell Your Child ***"I LOVE YOU"***

(continued)

327. Lead the family devotions at breakfast.
328. Help your son or daughter prepare to lead a family devotional time.
329. Have lunch together in the school cafeteria.
330. Turn off the TV and play a game together.

365 Ways to Tell Your Child *"I LOVE YOU"*

(continued)

331. Take advice from your kids, and encourage them to give it freely, even when it is confronting and personal.
332. Volunteer to help out when your child's class at school takes on a special project.
333. For a time of reflection together, ask your child: "What qualities do you value most in a friend?"

"I know my blackboard has had some bad marks, but it sure makes me feel good to know God has erased them. I'd always be in a bad mood if I didn't know my sins from yesterday are now gone. It's very, very important for me to know this. Without this part I could never go to heaven.

"I know God will never turn His back on me. One of my favorite verses is Romans 5:8 — 'But the proof of God's amazing love is this, in that while we were yet sinners Christ died for us.' God must love us a lot to let His Son die so that we won't have to go around feeling guilty, and then die and not make it to heaven.

"Jesus went through a lot of pain on the cross. They put a crown of thorns on His head. They whipped Him and made Him carry His own cross up to the hill where He was to die. However, He must have felt good inside knowing He was forgiving a lot of people.

"I don't know any other way that God could have proved how much He loves me. He must really love us a lot to forgive us like that!"

"as we forgive those who trespass against us ('our debtors')..."

"We've got to forgive others who are mean to us, who call us names, and who make us feel bad. We can't hold a grudge; we've got to erase it out of our minds, just as God does for us. If God loves us enough to forgive us, we've got to love our friends enough to forgive them, too.

365 Ways to Tell Your Child *"I LOVE YOU"*

(continued)

334. Say "I love you" — even *after* your child has volunteered you to make *all* the costumes for his class in the Christmas play at school.
335. When your child finishes last (or not much better) in a race or other contest — make a big display of encouragement and approval, because you know he was doing his best.

"One day last year I got in a fight with my friend, and I said I'd never invite her over to my house again. But after 'erasing' what she did to hurt me, I talked with her when I saw her again, and we were best friends again.

"If we don't forgive others, then God won't forgive us. The two come together like peanut butter and jelly. When your parents make you mad, or when you don't get something you want, that's when you've got to start praying and forgiving. If you don't, you won't want to be around them, and your relationship dies. You'll be scared of them and want to run away.

"Once Mom yelled at me for something I didn't think I did, but got blamed for. I really got mad. I felt like she didn't love me because I always get the blame. Then I forgave her and asked God to forgive me. I felt better, but I was still holding a grudge, so I talked to her about it. In a couple of days I forgot about it. I knew again that she's the best mom around, and I love her a lot."

"Lead us not into temptation..."

"When you want to do something that you know you shouldn't, God helps you to say no and to stay out of trouble.

"I like gymnastics, and to me getting victory over temptation is a lot like staying on the balance beam. When you try to do a cartwheel, back walkover, or forward roll, you've got to work hard to stay on the beam. In life, God is the one who keeps us on the right path. He keeps us on the beam, and helps us not to fall. Satan is the one who tempts us. He tries to make us hurt, and I'm just glad God helps me stay away from Satan's temptations."

"but deliver us from evil..."

"God helps us know what not to do by cautioning us through His Word. A few years ago, one of our two black labrador dogs saved the other one from drowning. God does the same thing for us when He delivers us from evil. The way God delivers us from evil is by giving us a good mind for understanding and deciding to follow what we see in His Word.

"For example, the passage that says 'Children, obey your parents' is one of the most important Bible verses for you or me. Your parents will help you do what is right; they've 'been there' before, and know what's best and safest for us, and what we need to avoid. We are to respect our parents, which means to think highly of them, to look up to them.

"One day Daddy bought a trampoline and moved it into our house. I was so excited about it that I started doing flips on it. Daddy cautioned me not to do flips yet, and, sure enough, when I did another one I fell off the trampoline and broke my wrist.

365 Ways to Tell Your Child ***"I LOVE YOU"***

(continued)

336. *Smile* at your child.
337. When your child's friends need an adult (besides their parents) to talk to — *be there.*
338. Take time to make today *special.*
339. Make smiley-face pancakes.

"Our parents are real strict about our television viewing because of all the weird things that are shown and said, and the way it can influence you to do weird things. It's amazing nowadays how even cartoons show witches and things like ghosts and creatures that represent Satan. Even toy makers have toys that represent Satan, like dead people living in coffins.

"As we ask God to deliver us from evil, we must remember that He has told us so much about what things to stay away from.

"God watches over us. He's always there to keep us safe. Whenever I hear a strange noise at night, I pray and ask God to keep our family safe. Usually I go right back to sleep."

"For Thine is the kingdom and the power and the glory forever..."

"God is the King of Kings. Our life is in His hands. I have a friend named Kim who sings a song entitled "In Your Hands." The song says that things will work out best in God's hands. He knows what is best.

"God has all the power in the world. He can bring a Christian back to life when he dies. He created the universe — it didn't just happen, but God Himself made it by just speaking it into being, and He made man by simply breathing into a lump of clay. No human being

365 Ways to Tell Your Child ***"I LOVE YOU"***

(continued)

340. Select a mentally challenging book (for both of you), and read it through together, pressing ahead to the end no matter how difficult.
341. Keep updated photos of your child around your home and office. Point them out to him often, and remark how you smile inside each time you see them.

365 Ways to Tell Your Child ***"I LOVE YOU"***

(continued)

342. For a time of reflection together, ask your child: "Who do you consider your greatest heroes?"
343. As you're working on a project that must be done by an adult, provide a scaled-down version of it that your child can do alongside you. Compliment him for the "good hands" God gave him.

could have ever done that. We aren't here on this earth just by chance. We were created by God's power, and that makes us special.

"My favorite T-shirt says, 'God Rules.' His reign on earth will be total when Christ returns. We should glorify Him now just like we will do then. We need to praise Him and tell Him that He is great, and that what He has done is good. Build Him up! It makes Him feel good to know we have our minds focused on His kingdom and power and glory. For this I give Him all the praise and honor in my life."

"Amen."

"When I say 'Amen' at the end of a prayer, it means, 'God, I agree with this prayer; it is true and right.' When I say 'Amen,' I tell God I believe He is right, and I thank Him for giving me this prayer to pray as I go to sleep each night."

PART FOUR

FOR HUSBAND & WIFE

SUBMIT! (BUT LOOK WHO GOT THE CAR!)

I PROMISE I was only kidding!

To appreciate the joke, you have to know Debbie Jo. My wife is secure, independent, quick-witted, and lovely. She works like a corporate president, thinks like a computer, and loves people energetically.

When I gave her a minivan last Christmas (with plenty of room to accommodate her four ever-growing children) and she saw the simple word "SUBMIT" on the personalized license plate, she burst out with laughter. " 'Submit' is what it says," she quickly noted, "but look who gets the car!"

Our lives have been intertwined since the first day my eyes caught Debbie Jo's eighteen years ago. Since day one we've repeatedly argued, cried, laughed, kidded, joked, fought, made up, grappled, and forgiven.

Debbie Jo is as strong as they come. When new junior-higher Courtney queried, "Mom, how much did *you* drink in college?" Debbie Jo said without batting an eye, *"None."* I knew it was the truth, even though her S.M.U. cheerleading days were filled with social fun.

I love her today like never before. It has never been easy for two independent, hard-headed people to live in harmony, but I wouldn't trade one crazy day with this brown-eyed classic for a lifetime with all the other beauties in the world.

Again this year she's taken long, deliberate strides toward becoming a better wife and mom. I respect her greatly for that. Our recent anniversary celebration was picture-postcard perfect. In fact, each of our anniversaries has been special in its own way.

My how I love that girl!

365 Ways to Tell Your Child **"I LOVE YOU"**

(continued)

344. The next time you make a special meal, allow your child to prepare one of the dishes (on his own, as much as possible). Serve and enjoy it with sincere praise for this young one's developing skills.
345. Talk with each other about your favorite books, and why you like them.

When the Bible tells hubbies, "Love your wives as Christ loved the church," it means listen to her, believe in her, sacrifice in every way for her, understand her, be patient with her, make her *feel* like a bride with first-class beauty. This kind of love is not a burden! It's the most exciting challenge of a man's life!

When the Bible finishes the puzzle and says, "Wives, submit to your husbands as unto the Lord," it isn't talking about slavery (as many modern thinkers would have you believe!). To submit to him means to encourage him each day as he enters the house. It means to build up his fragile ego, to honor him by listening to his ideas, to share your feelings with kindness, and to pray for him if he's not listening. Trust God for the end results to be right.

"Love never fails," the Bible claims boldly. *Never* is a long time. It's also an absolute.

Some men are harder to follow than others. Some women are harder to sacrifice for than others. But God made them — *all* of them — and following the instructions in His book *always* gets the end results.

Love never, never, never fails!

The harmony Debbie Jo and I experience doesn't come down "natural" or "easy." The process is not always fun and playful. We summarize the secret of our harmony with one word: *forgiveness* — a forgiveness bathed with mutual respect.

365 Ways to Tell Your Child "I LOVE YOU"

(continued)

346. When your child talks to you — be quiet, and use total concentration to listen. Put down what you're doing and look into his eyes. Maintain an encouraging expression, and when you speak, make your comments positive.
347. At your very next opportunity, give your child a hug. If he is younger, pick him up and hold him.

Last night we flared up at each other. Later, in my best British airs, I took her a cup of hot tea. We sipped tea together and made a joke out of the misunderstanding, and offered apologies.

ONE LEADERSHIP, TWO LEADERS

MY MOTIVATION in family relationships includes both Debbie Jo's honor and our kids' encouragement. And that means Debbie Jo and I need to be in agreement about our parenting policies. Our kids need only one family leadership *structure*, though it's a shared, two-person leadership.

On a recent Friday night I joined a searching mother and father who had placed their rebellious teenage boy in our youth home. These parents had it all. They were rich, attractive, and healthy, and their home had all the right trappings. Their trouble was that they weren't willing to submit to each other in the area of parenting. So the boy had two independent parental forces attempting to shape his life — and he fought the confusion like crazy. Fortunately, he's developing nicely now.

I have two nephews whose mom and dad are living on opposite sides of Texas from each other (and that's a long ways). Although times have been tough and the divorce a hurtful thing, that mom and dad have dedicated themselves to work together in their parenting, and to complement each other with direction for those two boys. You've got to respect that!

LOOKING LIKE AN ANGEL

HE WAS RUNNING AWAY from his wife, his home, and his family when he came by to bring me the news first-hand. Sam had been married for at least twelve years to a wonderful wife who had given him two of the finest children I've ever met. As the years wore on the charm wore off. Sam's mind told him this was a signal that he no longer loved his wife.

Man to man and eye to eye, we talked about love, about commitment, and about the strange mixture of emotion, passion, beauty, pride, and right and wrong that weave their way into the network of a relationship.

"Sam, why do you want to leave?" I asked.

"I just don't love her anymore. There's nothing left." Then he mumbled shamefully, "I really haven't loved her for a long time."

"What is love?" I asked him.

"I don't know any more. But whatever it is, it just isn't there."

He seemed totally convinced he was right. He went on: "You see, she's not beautiful to me — know what I mean? I'm not attracted to her at all."

I knew I had to venture onto shaky ground. "Sam, she's not beautiful to you because you don't treat her like a beautiful person. You give her leftovers, man. If you

365 Ways to Tell Your Child **"I LOVE YOU"**

(continued)

348. When your child says, "Watch me!" — watch him. Clap and cheer, and say, "Great job!"
349. Take regular ten-minute walks outdoors with your child — daily if possible, or at least once or twice a week. Allow the sense of wonder in his heart to unfold, as you observe God's creation.

treat a girl like a dog, she'll begin to look like one. You treat her like an angel and she begins to look like an angel. Trust me!"

I watched him bristle. "Well, she doesn't treat me good, either. She doesn't love me like she ought to."

"Sam, how much do you think she loves herself after the way you've been treating her lately?"

"I don't know. Not too much, I reckon."

"Can she give you what she doesn't have herself?"

"No, I suppose she can't."

We talked on for a couple of hours. He heard me with his ears, but his will still said "Leave her." And so he did.

Late one night four days later my phone rang.

"Joe, this is Sam. Guess where I am."

I was almost scared to guess. "An apartment?"

"No, I'm home. This time to stay. I knew you were right the other day, but I left anyway. I was away for three days but those were the worst three days of my life. I knew I had to go home."

After we talked, I choked up as I put down the phone.

A week later I saw Sam. "Guess what?" he asked with a grin as big as a Texas watermelon.

"You're in love," I ventured a guess.

"Yep, but that's not all."

"What else?"

365 Ways to Tell Your Child ***"I LOVE YOU"***

(continued)

350. Each time you greet your child, do it eagerly and warmly.
351. Ask your child, "What new hobbies would you most like to try getting into?
352. Write to your children whenever they're away. Send cards with messages of encouragement.
353. Make personalized Christmas tree ornaments together.

365 Ways to Tell Your Child "I LOVE YOU"

(continued)

354. Save ten percent of your energy from your work day, and take it home with you to spend on your children and spouse. Offer your best to your family.
355. If your child especially dislikes one of his chores, think of a surprising way to make it more fun.
356. *Listen* very hard — even when your ears are tired!

His eyes danced with playful emotion. "Guess who is the most beautiful girl I know?"

"I'm not sure, Sam."

"My wife. You were right. She's gotten so much more attractive since I began to love her and treat her like I ought to."

Sam was one of the few who return. He's the lucky one. I was so proud of him I could have squeezed his neck off.

PART FIVE

JUST FOR KIDS

THE RAREST TREASURE

IN THE VICINITY of Ali Haged's farm in Southern Iran, an ancient legend is still told by a local Persian wise man:

"In the beginning, the earth was first a giant ball of fire that the Almighty spun vigorously with his finger and released with great speed into the expanse of the Universe. As the fiery ball of molten mass burned its way through space it intercepted giant banks of fog, which condensed and mixed furiously on the earth's surface, cooling the outer crust. As the earth's surface cooled, internal fiery lava burst through the crust, and instantly mountains and valleys and canyons and oceans were formed."

The wise man concludes his story with this intriguing thought, one that has been handed down through countless generations (and which has lured many an unguided nomad away from home in search of great riches): "The material which cooled most quickly turned into limestone. The material more reluctant to cool turned into silver. That which cooled even less quickly became gold. And finally, the slowest particles to cool became diamonds... the most valuable gems on earth."

Diamonds and other such precious stones are presented to lovers in moments of highest honor. I gave a diamond engagement ring to my little honey in a Cracker Jack box, while we were high on a mountain looking over a cliff. But the Cracker Jacks were stale, and she started to throw the box over the edge as I screamed: "Wait, the surprise! Look for the surprise!" (Fortunately she found it...and still wears it today.)

But a gem more precious than a diamond — and far more rare to behold — is found in the magic when a son or daughter breathes an encouraging word or deed to a parent whose heart is long overdue for a lift.

The teenage boy scoffs at his daddy's antique ideas and balding head. Then twenty years rush by, and the teenager's hairline has started receding — and *his* kid beleaguers him with jeers of disobedience.

What goes around, comes around.

Bald daddies have bald sons.

Selfish mothers have selfish daughters.

Ornery kids have ornery kids.

Neat kids who shower their parents with love and honor tend to have neat kids who shower them with love and honor.

I've seen it from both sides...countless hundreds of times.

Encouragement Always Wins

BROOKE WAS SEVENTEEN when she came to me protesting about her distant, non-understanding father: "Joe, all my problems are because of him. I can't stand this man. The way he treats me and my mom — you wouldn't believe this guy. He has me totally frustrated and confused. My life is becoming a wreck."

I let the ball bounce in her court. "Brooke, would you like to see him change? To become a wonderful man again?"

"No way. It's impossible. You don't know how stubborn he is."

"Brooke, you can change that man. Encouragement always wins."

She squirmed. "Not with him it doesn't."

I persisted. As I kept talking, Brooke's brown eyes began to sparkle with creativity.

In the next twelve hours, she developed a plan that startled me with its creativity and depth. She wrote the following list of specific goals for how to encourage her Dad over the next twelve months.

1. Once a week, ask Dad to wake up early with me so we can pray together for our family.
2. Help Dad paint the house.
3. Once a week, make him a nutritious snack to take to the office.
4. Stock his refrigerator at his office with nutritional munchies once every two weeks.
5. Serve him breakfast in bed once every two weeks.
6. Once a month, offer to go up to his office with him to help him get caught up on any work, clean for him, etc.
7. Ask him to spend time with me going over college material.
8. Tell him "I love you" every day.
9. Give him specific compliments every day.
10. Hug him every day.
11. Offer to do the grocery shopping once every two weeks.
12. Take out the trash (collect, bag, etc.) twice a week.
13. Don't ask for any money for "fun things."
14. Make time to talk to him every day.
15. Ask him to have Bible study or devotions with me once a week.
16. Send him a note with just the words, "I love you! Love, Brooke."
17. Give him a blown-up picture of myself with a big sign that says, "I love you, Daddy."
18. Send him a letter with a friendship bracelet enclosed.
19. Make him a painted T-shirt.
20. Fix and serve him dinner with all his favorite foods.
21. Play miniature golf together.
22. Make a list of all the qualities that I admire in him and want to have.
23. Take over the yard work (mow, rake, trim, etc.).

24. Help him plan a special surprise for Mom.
25. Write him a poem.
26. Buy a watermelon, take Dad to the park, and have a watermelon eating and seed-spitting contest.
27. "Kidnap" him from his office one day during lunch, and take him on a picnic.
28. Go in and decorate his office with streamers and posters, with a big banner hanging that says, "My Dad is Number One."
29. Write him a Bible verse every day, tape it to his steering wheel, and talk to him about it when he gets home.
30. Make a list of some of the major things he has done for me, and why I appreciate each one.
31. Ask him to help me make a list of the qualities I need to look for in dates and my future mate.
32. Take him out to lunch and pick up the bill.

Three months later my phone rang. A familiar teenage voice spoke with excitement. "Hi, it's Brooke. Guess what? It's working!"

Three months later she called again. "Hello, it's me again. Guess who my new best friend is?"

Back at our camp the next summer, a happy, teary-eyed Brooke brought me this letter from her newly discovered Daddy:

> Brooke, today as I was traveling on the plane I saw a little girl. She reminded me of you when you were younger. I began to think about how much I appreciated you, not so much for all the things you have done but for the person that you are. Brooke, I admire that person and I love that person…your love has also shown your Mom and I how to love each other better.
>
> I'm proud to be your Daddy.

Awaiting Discovery

EVERY HOME HAS a treasure chest or two ready to be opened. Some are balding, some are graying. Most have wrinkled faces from years of long nights and hard days. They have callused hands from countless hours of labor providing a home for their sons and daughters. The moms have circles beneath their eyes when their makeup washes off, as a result of countless nights rocking or pacing the floor with a sick child, and waiting up for a teenage girl to come home from a date. The dads have callused knees from many prayerful nights and hundreds of "Dad, you be the horsy" games. Their backs don't straighten completely due to decades of time bent over an office desk, a steering wheel, or a pick and shovel.

They don't ask much in return. The ones who expect it usually end up disappointed.

Parents. They're the wisest of the wise, the humblest of the humble, the givingest of the givers, and the most unappreciated people on earth.

The treasure chest is opened to the child who says, "Hey, Dad, you're the best." Or, "You know, Mom, some day I hope to be as lovely as you are."

Our peppy little middle child, Courtney, wrote her mom such a note recently. Debbie Jo carries it in her Bible for safekeeping. It's a ten-karat gem:

> Dear Mom,
>
> Thank you for always being there when I need you. And always building me up. You are the best Mom in the world! I would not trade you in for $1,000,000,000,000.
>
> Love always, Courtney

Last summer a seventeen-year-old Billy Idol look-alike stepped off a charter bus and into our camp. He had been high on acid for three days prior to his departure. His Dad was near the end of his rope.

As the early days of camp passed, this boy with three-colored hair and a drug-riddled body came to grips with his dead-end pathway. At the end of the second week in his Ozark home, surrounded by an ocean of legitimate Christians who had painted for him a new picture of existence, he wrote his Dad the following letter.

> I'm sorry, Dad, for the traumas I've caused in the family. The drug scene became more serious than I ever planned, and it got out of control. I'm sorry. At first, I saw you feel guilt of some sort, and confusion. None, and I mean none, of that stuff was the least bit your responsibility. I was old enough to make the decisions I made involving the drugs and I made the wrong choice.
>
> Dad, I don't know if it would be possible for anyone to care too much, but you would certainly be that person if it was. You burden yourself with so much responsibility and duty and concern. And I know that I'm not the first person to tell you that. And I say it not only as son to father, but as person to person, friend to friend. Dad, you're awesome.
>
> Only now am I beginning to appreciate all that you did for me as I was growing up. And at the same time, I'm learning that, rather than doing things my way, I need to put my trust in your word and advice.
>
> Thanks, Dad, I love you. Happy Father's Day to not only the "best Dad in the whole world," but to my best friend.

His Daddy came to life. Treasure chest reopened. Diamond discovered. Layers of hurt peeled away. A boy had found his dad again.

Encouragement always wins.

Shannon's dad spent eight years battling a Goliath in the courtroom. The stakes were high. Bankruptcy and embarrassment loomed with a tap from the judge's gavel. In the final week of the trial, the father found a "magic feather," a note from the creative pen of his "teenage queen" who had discovered life's richest secret. On his way to court he read the note:

> I'm so proud of you, Daddy! You've come so far and waited too long, and now it's finally here. The day we plead our case and fight for justice.
>
> I want you to know that there is absolutely no one else on this earth that I respect and admire more than you. You have the endurance of an immortal, the mind of a genius, a heart of gold, and the love of Jesus.
>
> If we were not to gain a single cent from this trial, I couldn't care. I will love, admire and respect you all the more because you're always THE BEST to me. I will stand behind you in everything you do and say during the trial and after it — because I believe in you.
>
> We have the force of tons of people praying for us and I know that today is going to be a GREAT DAY!
>
> I LOVE YOU DADDY!
>
> Princess

Your dad will never be fifty-seven again. Your mom's hour-glass of time is quickly passing into its final years. If you're fortunate, you'll have a jolly grandparent to bring your child home to. But having to look back and say, "I wish I had only taken time to..." is *so* painful. Funerals are full of "If only's."

So go ahead...
and take time...
to discover a diamond.

W R A P - U P

A WISH

Feast for My Eyes

BRINGING UP FOUR CHILDREN has without a doubt been the biggest challenge of my life. Many times I've felt like I did the day I brought home my third-grade report card with the equivalent of two D's. I felt like a failure then...and as a dad, I still do many times. But you know what? It's worth the battle when a dad gets a day like today. Today has been a feast for my forty-year-old eyes.

With me are my two daughters, those two little female packages who still say "Daddy" like it all began yesterday. The ocean spray blows across the paper on which I now write. We are on the Sea of Cortez, off the Baja coast of Mexico, thirty miles from LaPaz. This is the most beautiful scuba diving water in the world.

Today we've been diving with (and I mean *with*) sea lions. A hundred of these curious creatures have been playing with our fins and snorkels like a preschool class attacking a new box of Legos.

My junior-high and high-school daughters are in kid paradise. I'm taking pictures like crazy. The squeals of excitement would reach the coast if they weren't muffled by diving masks and mouthpieces. This is one of those Daddy-kid experiences that comes once in a lifetime.

The aquarium in which we dive is so beautiful, so natural, so undisturbed — an unparalleled expression of

*365 Ways to Tell Your Child **"I LOVE YOU"***

(continued)

357. Keep your home open to your children's friends, and treat them the way you treat your own kids.
358. Be a "note fairy": Place an encouraging note under your child's pillow while he sleeps, to be found in the morning.
359. Ask your child what achievements and accomplishments in life he is proudest of.

365 Ways to Tell Your Child *"I LOVE YOU"*

(continued)

360. For your daughter, make a special outfit (Easter is a great occasion for this) instead of buying something new.
361. Color Easter eggs together — make each egg a personalized masterpiece.
362. Climb the roof together to get a good view of your city's Fourth-of-July fireworks display.

God's awesome handiwork. Spectacular fish surround us: multicolored starfish, green moray eels, king angel fish, spotted puffer fish, neon gobies, and a thousand other species.

As we dive through a giant school of porpoises in some rough, deep water (dangerous territory for a four-foot-eight pipsqueak), my novice junior-high girl is keeping up with the pros who've joined us. (Is it okay to tell you how proud I am of her right now?)

My girls have passed up so much of the world's entertainment as they've made difficult social stands in their growing up years, but today it's all worth the sacrifice. This undersea spectacular is a backdrop for two young lives in scuba gear, lives that are every bit as unspoiled, every bit as beautiful as the scenery around them. Today there is no peer pressure dragging them down, no guilt, no shame — nothing to interfere with a grateful dad embracing the wind.

Back in the states, moms and dads are attending committee meetings, business seminars, adult social gatherings, and a thousand other grown-up activities, while their kids spend evenings in front of the TV with the sitter. Based on today's standards of priorities as measured in *GQ* and *Mademoiselle* magazine, I guess Debbie Jo and I are a little nutty about our children. Our social calendar is pretty much filled with soccer camps, school band concerts, and gymnastics meets — and, thankfully, spectacular moments like today.

NOW AS I WRITE, we're flying over the California border. It always feels so wonderful to see America again after a visit away. I breathe a deep sigh. In the distance I see the full moon's reflection on the salty sea. Yet the silver glow doesn't begin to match the shining wonder reflected by the blessed nation now filling the view below us. We've got it all down there! We've got freedom to raise our kids in the right way, with no fear of governmental intervention. We have comfortable homes. We have food on the table. We are, indeed, the world's most blessed nation.

As the plane touches down, I wonder: Will my kids have the opportunity to enjoy with their kids the kind of day I've enjoyed today? If the current moral deterioration continues, I believe our days are numbered. The Romans, Greeks, and Egyptians couldn't handle the kind of abundant days that we're now enjoying. The adults fell into corruption, and the kids followed like children after the Pied Piper.

I see an evening star out my window...if it were to fall, and if there were such a thing as wishes-come-true, I'd wish that in the future your kids, my kids, and every American kid could have a day like today with their own children — in fact, lots of them. And I'd wish that each one of those kids could look back and say truthfully that they received from us the precious gift of self-esteem.

365 Ways to Tell Your Child ***"I LOVE YOU"***

(continued)

363. Help your child raise a farm animal.
364. For a time of reflection together, ask each other: "How do you picture heaven?"
365. As you talk to your children today, say the three magic words *"I LOVE YOU."* You've earned credibility — and they'll believe you!

Jehovah is our God, Jehovah alone.
You must love him with *all* your heart, soul, and might.
And you must think constantly about these commandments
I am giving you today. You must teach them to your children
and talk about them when you are at home or out for a walk;
at bedtime and the first thing in the morning...

Deuteronomy 6:4-7, *The Living Bible*

THIRTY FAMILY DEVOTIONALS

These devotional readings — written by myself and my family and friends, including campers and staff members at Kanakuk and Kanakomo youth camps — are designed to help guide ALL your family in a month's worth of rich daily times together with the Lord and His Word.

❑

DAY 1

ENCOURAGEMENT

by MICHELLE MIDDLETON

Many times people do not realize (as God does) the power of an encouraging word. Encouragement can help someone through a struggle, give someone that extra boost of strength to persevere, or make someone's day. Giving encouragement may not be the easiest thing to do toward someone you don't know very well or someone with whom you don't get along. But you never know how God may use your words to help someone.

Hebrews 10:24-25 shows the importance of encouragement in Christian fellowship: "And let us consider how we may spur on one another to love and good deeds. Let us not give up meeting together, as some are in the habit of doing, but let us encourage one another — and all the more as we see the Day approaching."

I received the following poem from a friend. It really drove the point home for me! I put a copy of it in my locker at school to remind me to spur on my friends every day.

AT DAY'S END
(by John Hall)

Is anyone happier because you passed his way?
Does anyone remember that you spoke to him today?
The day is almost over, and its toiling time is through;
Is there anyone to utter now a kindly word to you?
Can you say tonight, in parting with the day that's slipping fast,
That you've helped a single brother of the many that you've passed?
Is a single heart rejoicing over what you did or said?
Does the man whose hopes were fading, now with courage look ahead?
Did you waste the day or lose it? Was it well or sorely spent?
Did you leave a trail of happiness or a scar of discontent?
As you close your eyes in slumber, do you think that God will say,
"You've earned one more tomorrow by the work you did today"?

PRAYER FOR THE DAY:

Dear Lord, help me be sensitive to the needs of others. Use me to lift other people up instead of putting them down. Help me remember to keep a positive attitude in every situation. Give me encouragement, and remind me to do the same for those around me. In Jesus name, Amen.

DISCUSSION QUESTIONS:

1. What does God instruct us to do in Hebrews 10:24-25?
2. When should we encourage others? (Read Galatians 6:10.)
3. How are we urged to act toward others?
4. Can you think of a time when encouragement has made a difference to you — or *could* have made a difference to you?

THOUGHT FOR THE DAY:

Encouragement is like a mug of hot chocolate. It warms you from the inside out.

❑

DAY 2

ALWAYS

by SPIKE WHITE (MY DAD)

"I am with you always even unto the end of the world" (Matthew 28:30).

What a wonderful and comfortable and inspiring promise! We know it came from the lips and the heart of the greatest man who ever lived.

God in His glory reminds us daily of this promise. The

sun always rises on a regular and predictable schedule according to the season.The birds and butterflies migrate predictably by season. Watermelon seeds always produce watermelons and acorns always produce oak trees.

Our lives can be monuments to Jesus' promise if we pray, seek His will for every occasion, and reflect Him in all we do and say.

Prayer for the Day:

O God, we know you are always "handy." Help us take time to listen to your messages and then act on them.

Discussion Questions:

1. In what ways are we made aware of Christ's presence every day?
2. How does God show us His consistency and dependability?
3. When was the last time you really felt the nearness of Jesus?
4. How can we hear what God is telling us?

Thought for the Day:

"Hooray" for the sunrise and the opportunity to live this day to its fullest!

DAY 3

"BEE BEE BUMBLE BEE ALL'S OUT'S IN FREE!"

by DARNELL WHITE (MY MOM)

"For I know thy abode and thy going out and thy coming in" (2 Kings 19:27).

Back (w-a-y back!) when I was a kid, the best part of the day was late, late evening at dusk when we played outside after supper. Hide-and-Go-Seek was the all-time favorite game...plus Red Rover and Statues ("Freeze!")...and Ice Box. All the kids living anywhere within hollerin' distance would be "playing out" too. How we would beg: "Mom, can we stay out a little longer?"

Those were the good old days! I'm really glad we didn't have television then. We would have missed all that pure "cross-my-heart-and-hope-to-die" FUN.

Genesis 3 tells how mankind first sinned and fell out of harmony with God. I suppose you could say Adam played the first game of Hide-and-Go-Seek. And God called to Adam, "Where are you?" (Of course, God knew where Adam was, because He is sovereign and knows everything!) David wrote in Psalms 44:21, "Would not God find this out? For He knows the secret of the heart." But — how neat! — God loved Adam so much He cared to seek for Adam and call out, "Where are you?" God wants us to have an open relationship with Him — and not have to seek us as we hide somewhere because we feel guilty and ashamed to face Him.

When that Great Day dawns and the Lord returns, I think He will seek us like that again. And I want to be ready and "playing out," and hear Him call, "Bee Bee Bumble Bee, All's Out's in Free!"

PRAYER FOR THE DAY:

Dear God, thank You for loving me and knowing what I think in my heart and all I do when nobody else sees. Help me never hide from You, and to bow my knees and confess each sin. And thank You for letting me IN FREE!

DISCUSSION QUESTIONS:

1. Can you think of some ways that we play Hide-and-go-seek with God?
2. How can we communicate more openly with each other and with God?
3. How would you feel if you did something wrong and kept it a secret, then heard God's voice calling, "Where are You?"

THOUGHT FOR THE DAY:

The true measure of holiness is what you do when no one but God is watching.

❑

DAY 4

LITTLE BITTY SEEDS

by COURTNEY WHITE (MY DAUGHTER, AGE 11)

"And it came about that as he was sowing, some seed fell beside the road, and the birds came and ate it up. And other seed fell on the rocky ground where it did not have much soil; and immediately it sprang up because it had no depth of soil. And after the sun had risen, it was scorched; and because it had no root, it withered away. And other seed fell among the thorns, and the thorns came up and choked it, and it yielded no crop. And other seed fell into the good soil and as they grew up and increased, they yielded a crop and produced thirty, sixty, and one hundred fold" (Mark 4:3-8).

When the farmer spread his seeds, some seed fell in the road and the birds came and ate it up. God's Word is the seed. Sometimes it never goes through our ears and into our hearts. It is all too easy to have a hard heart that is full of sin. But a heart that's hard misses everything that's good.

Other seed fell on the rocky ground where it did not have much soil. Often people can hear the Word of God, but when they go home they forget God because they have no background for His Word.

Still other seed fell among the thorns, and the thorns came up and choked it, and it yielded no crop. This person grew a little after hearing the Word, but he let peer pressure choke the Word and soon he was following the crowd and doing things he shouldn't do.

And other seeds fell into the good soil, and as they grew up they increased and yielded a crop and produced thirty, sixty, and a hundred fold. That means that he became a strong Christian and told other people about Christ.

Prayer for the Day:

Dear Lord, thank You for giving me a home that makes my heart fertile soil. Help me to produce fruit in my life by listening to You and loving each person in my family as much as I love myself. Amen.

Discussion Questions:

1. What kind of ground are your seeds planted in? Why?
2. What are two things that keep your ground from being better soil?
3. What kind of soil are your friends? How can you help them have deeper soil?

Thought for the Day:

What you sow is what you get.

❑

DAY 5

FEARFULLY AND WONDERFULLY MADE

by SHARON DODD

"For Thou didst form my inward parts; Thou didst weave me in my mother's womb. I will give thanks to Thee, for I am fearfully and wonderfully made" (Psalm 139:13-15).

Did you know that God breathed His life into us, and that is how we came into this world? That is amazing to me. His breath is in me! Wow! He did not do that for any other creature.

What does all this mean? And do I truly believe it?

Have you ever thought things like these: "Cathy is so pretty; I wish I had her legs." "Bobby always has the latest gadgets." "Cindy's hair and makeup are always perfect." "Bill is on the football team and dates Cindy." On and on it goes. Are you happy with what God has given you? When we begin to compare ourselves with others we get into trouble. The grass is always greener on the other side. Did you ever stop to think that thoughts like these are a slap in God's face? You are saying that God really messed up with you. And did you realize that the person you are envious of is wishing he or she looked like someone else or had more than someone else has?

So get back to the Word of God. He made you just the way He wanted you to look, and He thinks you're beautiful! Besides, what does Psalm 139 say? "For Thou didst form my inward parts..." Are you beautiful in your spirit? Thank God for every aspect of you — inside to outside.

PRAYER FOR THE DAY:

Dear Jesus, forgive me when I wish for more of something that someone else has. Let me look at myself the way You do. Thank You for making me just the way You did. And I will let You develop me in Your way and in Your time.

Discussion Questions:

1. How often today have you compared yourself to someone else — mentally, physically, or spiritually?
2. Do you focus more on the outside or the inside?
3. Name five things about yourself that you can thank God for.

Thought for the Day:

Make Jesus your perspective. He — not the world — sets the standards for who and what we are! And He says that we are chosen, precious, wonderful. Remember, we were made with the Master's hand and it is His breath that we breath.

❑

Day 6

WHO THEN IS THIS MAN?

by Joe White

"And He is the image of the invisible God, the first-born of all creation. For by Him all things were created, both in the heavens and on earth, visible and invisible, whether thrones or dominions or rulers or authorities — all things have been created by Him and for Him. And He is before all things, and in Him all things hold together. He is also head of the body, the church; and He is the beginning, the first-born from the dead; so that He Himself might come to have first place in everything. For it was the Father's good pleasure for all the fullness to dwell in Him..." (Colossians 1:15-19).

A few years ago I met a man who tried to sell me the line that Jesus wasn't God, that Jesus was just another man like you and me, that we are as much sons of God as Jesus was. Many cults make this same assertion. (*Time* magazine recently reported that an estimated 1,800 cults have been in operation in the last few years.)

If Jesus wasn't God, why did His close friend, John, write at the very start of his gospel, "In the beginning was the Word (Jesus) and the Word was with God and the Word was God"? And why did Jesus' friend Peter say to Him, "You are the Christ, the Son of the living God" (Matthew 16:16)?

At Christ's crucifixion, one of the centurions said, "Truly, this was the son of God!" (Matthew 27:54).

The apostle Paul — who along with ten of the twelve closest followers of Christ suffered a martyr's death because of his commitment to the fact that Jesus claimed to be God — wrote these words: "In Christ all the fullness of the Deity dwells in bodily form" (Colossians 2:9).

Most convincing of all, Jesus stuck by His claim to be God until the bitter end. He was killed in the most tortuous fashion after He insisted at His trial, "I am the Christ, the Son of God." They called it blasphemy, and He was crucified for it.

Prayer for the Day:

Thanks be to God for the indescribable gift of Jesus, His Son.

Discussion Questions:

1. Jesus said to Peter, "Who do you say that I am?" The same question is yours today: Who do you say He is?
2. Where would we be if "the visible image of the invisible God" hadn't been revealed to us in Jesus Christ?

Thought for the Day:

Just as water is H_2O, and just as an apple is composed of seed, fruit, and peel — so God expresses Himself as Father, Son, and Holy Spirit.

Day 7

FATHERLY FOCUS

by Trey Moore

"Therefore, since we have so great a cloud of witnesses surrounding us, let us also lay aside every encumbrance, and the sin which so easily entangles us, and let us run with endurance the race that is set before us, fixing our eyes on Jesus, the author and perfecter of faith, who for the joy set before Him endured the cross, despising the shame, and has sat down at the right hand of the throne of God" (Hebrews 12:1-2).

We need to stay away from the people, places, and thoughts that cause us to stumble and fall away from our ultimate goal: that of becoming more like Jesus Christ. To be able to "throw off everything that hinders," we have to keep our mind focused on Christ and His plan.

For instance, when we go to school each day, we can't leave Christ outside. We can't "run with perseverance" unless, when we feel like quitting and giving up, we remember that Jesus endured ten times the pain we feel.

In the summer before I went into ninth grade, my family moved from Dallas to Chicago. I didn't want to move; I didn't understand why we had to move. In my anger, I prayed we would move back to Dallas. That year in Chicago, I struggled in my walk with Christ more than ever before. If my mind had been focused on Jesus and His plan for me, I would have known that He had a reason for me being in Chicago. After I realized this, I began to hang on and not give up so easily. My walk with the Lord has been strengthened tremendously.

If we keep our eyes fixed on Christ and never give up the struggle to become more like Christ, we can achieve amazing things, whether in school or sports, or something in our relationships with our family and peers.

Prayer for the Day:

Lord, we ask You today for wisdom. Help us to see You and Your desires more clearly, so we can do Your will. In Jesus' name, Amen.

Discussion Questions:

1. Have you ever let your selfishness or anger get the best of you? When?
2. Have you ever tried to focus your eyes on two things at once — one of them near at hand and the other far away? How can we shift our focus from ourselves to Christ?

Thought for the Day:

When you pray today, instead of asking God to help you, think of someone you know who is having problems and ask God to help that person. Keep him or her on your prayer list.

❑

Day 8

DON'T GIVE UP

by Josh Putnam

"And let us not lose heart in doing good, for in due time we shall reap if we do not grow weary. So then, while we have an opportunity, let us do good to all men, and especially to those who are of the household of faith" (Galatians 6:9-10).

In these two verses Paul told the church at Galatia to continue doing good by helping people and providing for the needs of the church. He promised them they would be rewarded if they endured in the tasks given to them and didn't give up. He also exhorted them to seize every opportunity to help others. We are supposed to give of ourselves, putting God first, others second, and self third. That is the "I'm Third" life. Verse nine says we will reap a harvest if we don't give up. The reward might not come right away, but eventually we will be blessed. It may be bittersweet, it may not turn out the way you wanted it to, but God knows best and He hasn't given up on us. Your blessing will eventually come: thirty, sixty, or a hundred fold.

In the first game of our season-ending basketball tournament last year, this verse about not quitting really came to life for me. We were playing a very tough opponent. Going into the fourth quarter our team was down by twenty points, and one of our starters had fouled out. It would have been easy to quit and give up all hopes of getting to the championship. We chose to give 110 percent, and as a result tied the game and went on to win in overtime. We didn't win the tournament, but we saw in that first game how God rewards those who don't give up.

We can easily see how these two verses apply to everyday life. For example, if an acquaintance at school is gossiping about you or keeps giving you a bad time — pray for him, don't return evil for evil. Even if he keeps it up, do not give up. Jesus didn't.

These verses can be applied to situations with parents, teachers, and brothers and sisters. If results don't show right away, be patient. God is in control and He will reward you for your perseverance.

Prayer for the Day:

Jesus, thank You for never quitting on us. You gave everything You had until the very end. Help us to never give up in doing good. Amen.

Discussion Questions:

1. Tell about a time you felt like quitting when you were trying to do good to someone else, but it seemed hopeless. Did you keep trying? What happened?
2. Where would we be if Jesus had quit when it got tough for Him?
3. How can we apply this verse in our lives today?

Thought for the Day:

We can always win! If we give 110 percent and look to Him — we'll smile in the end.

❑

Day 9

HONOR AND OBEY

by Nathan Firestone

"Children, obey your parents in the Lord, for this is right. Honor your father and mother (which is the first commandment with a promise), that it may be well with you, and that you may live long on the earth. And, fathers, do not provoke your children to anger; but bring them up in the discipline and instruction of the Lord" (Ephesians 6:1-4).

This passaage is about the arrangement God made for families, and the responsibilities parents and children have to each other. It's important to me because it helps me remember God's plan for the family. When I receive instruction or discipline from my parents, often I don't like it. Sometimes I think it's unfair. It's difficult to obey. But I believe that if I practice being obedient to my parents now, it will be easier to be obedient to Christ throughout my life.

I try to be honest with my parents and follow their instructions. But there have been some times (and there will be more) when I'm tempted to do something that I know they don't want me to.

Recently two of my friends and I were out walking one evening. They asked me to go with them to a party at the home of a guy from my school who has lots of parties at his house on weekends. My mom had encouraged me not to become close friends with this boy because of the influence he might have on me.

I said, "I better not go because my mom wouldn't want me to." They said, "Come on, she'll never even know." I ended up walking home by myself. I didn't want my parents to lose their trust in me. Sure, it would have been easy to go on to the party. My parents probably wouldn't have found out. I know that if I had lied in this small incident, I would have found it easier and easier to get in the habit of lying.

I think all teenagers can benefit from following these passages to help make a better family life and develop a good relationship with their parents. Many of us, as teenagers, want to be free to make our own decisions and do what we want. But if we truly love the Lord, we will put His will before our own.

I know it's hard to be obedient, but remember that the two key words *Honor* and *Obey* are Christ's instructions for us.

Prayer for the Day:

Dear Lord, teach me to be obedient and help me to listen to my parents at all times, as they listen to You. Amen.

Discussion Questions:

1. When do you find it most difficult to obey your parents? Why?
2. Do you sometimes struggle with being obedient to Christ? When?

THOUGHT FOR THE DAY:

Today I'll give up my desires for Christ's desires, and seek His wisdom through my parents.

❑

DAY 10

HELP IN HARD TIMES

by BLAKE DOBBE

"I cry aloud with my voice to the LORD;
I make supplication with my voice to the LORD.
I pour out my complaint before Him;
I declare my trouble before Him.
When my spirit was overwhelmed within me,
Thou didst know my path.
In the way where I walk
They have hidden a trap for me.
Look to the right and see;
For there is no one who regards me;
There is no escape for me;
No one cares for my soul.
I cried out to Thee, LORD;
I said, "Thou art my refuge,
My portion in the land of the living.
Give heed to my cry,
For I am brought very low;
Deliver me from my persecutors,
For they are too strong for me.
Bring my soul out of prison,
So that I may give thanks to Thy name;
The righteous will surround me,
For thou wilt deal bountifully with me."

(Psalm 142)

This passage of Scripture shows victory where there seems to be no hope of survival. It tells us to rely on God in all situations. It reminds us that He is always there for us. This psalm is an encouragement to me because it emphasizes all that I need, all that I want, and all that I live for: Jesus Christ!

This year I've been going through some very rough family problems. As a way of encouraging me during this tough time, two school basketball players jotted down Psalm 142 on a piece of paper and gave it to me. Their thoughtfulness lifted my spirits as much as the Scripture itself.

I realized I have to proceed past my family problems with my own life, relying completely on Jesus. He never fails to give me His best. He is continually blessing my life. My relationship with Him is stronger than ever and this psalm sparked it! My problems aren't solved, but I know they are in God's hands and that He'll take care of everything in His own special way.

Prayer for the Day:

Dear Lord, thank You for always being there for me. I especially appreciate You, Lord, for being with me in my toughest times. Help me turn to You when I need that special Someone to lean on. In my Savior's name I pray, Amen.

Discussion Questions:

1. Who are the people you trust the most? Are there certain people you rely on in more difficult circumstances? Is there someone you can trust with any situation?
2. Do you have a friend who might feel helpless or alone right now? Would Psalm 142 encourage this person?
3. Describe the time when you felt you needed God more than anyone else and more than at any other time.

Thought for the Day:

God is at His best when you need Him the most.

Day 11

SEEING CLEARLY

by Julie Primrose

"When I was a child, I used to speak as a child, think as a child, reason as a child; when I became a man, I did away with childish things. For now we see in a mirror dimly, but then face to face; now I know in part, but then I shall know fully just as I also have been fully known" (1 Corinthians 13:11-12).

This passage relates childhood to our understanding of God's will. It helps us realize that we are not supposed to understand everything that happens, but we should be patient and take one step at a time. Then later, when the time is right, God reveals to us His reason.

When my grandmother became ill with cancer, I could not figure out why God was letting this happen. Why did He permit my grandmother to experience so much pain? I asked this question many times, hoping God would realize He had made a mistake in allowing this godly woman to suffer so terribly. But instead of getting better, my grandmother got worse and then passed away.

Previously, my Sunday school teacher had shared this verse from 1 Corinthians with me. During Grandmother's illness God brought it back to mind. Even though I didn't understand her sickness and death, the verse made me realize there was a purpose in it, and that the situation would work out for the best. What could be better for her than to go home to be with the Lord and spend eternity in His kingdom?

When things like this happen, making it appear as though the sky might fall, remember that God knows everything that happens and He is going to take care of His children.

He gave us a promise in Romans saying that all things work together for good for those who love the Lord. This gives us a hope and a reassurance that the sky won't fall.

Prayer for the Day:

God, thank You that all things do work together for our good. We praise You for Your wisdom. Please give us contentment and peace in our hearts despite the questions in our minds when we don't see things clearly. Thank You that the day will come when we'll have the answers. Until then, we give our trust to You. Amen.

Discussion Questions:

1. Describe a situation when you felt like a child, not knowing or understanding what was going on around you.
2. Does God promise you immediate knowledge or immediate wisdom? Does He promise that you will have the answers in His time?

Thought for the Day:

God has a better way.

❑

Day 12

LET IT SHINE

by Ben Caswell

"You are the salt of the earth; but if the salt has become tasteless, how will it be made salty again? It is good for nothing any more, except to be thrown out and trampled under foot by men. You are the light of the world. A city set on a hill cannot be hidden. Nor do men light a lamp, and put it under the peck-measure, but on the lamp stand; and it gives light to all who are in the house. Let your light shine before men in such a way that they may see your good works, and glorify your Father who is in heaven" (Matthew 5:13-16).

Referring to Christians as lights in a dark world creates a beautiful and appropriate analogy. Matthew, in preserving Christ's words, conveys to us a vital message, which — like the city on the mountain — cannot be ignored.

To be effective lights in and for this world, to show people the proper way, we must always assume the responsibility God intends for us. A lamp reveals shape and form within a dark room, just as the abiding Christian gives direction and discernment in the world.

Some two thousand years ago, Jesus Christ made a path on earth; today it's up to us to determine whether His path will be lit up and seen, or whether the lost will continue to stumble in darkness.

As a high school junior I sometimes find myself forgetting how important being a light is. I get too busy at times and find that I have turned off my light. The above passage always helps me realize how much I owe to God.

I find at times that I misuse the light. I put myself in the light rather than God. But when I read this verse, it acts as a "humilifier" for me. What I mean by this made-up word is that the verse stresses the importance of humility: God should get the glory. So rather than just keeping the light on, I need to remember on whom the light should be focused. Matthew 5:16 is a good reminder.

Jesus counts on us to continue the journey He began long ago. Let's please Him by letting our lights shine. Happiness is the guaranteed result!

Prayer for the Day:

Dear God, thank You for being the light of my life. Help me to let Your light shine through so I can light up the path for others. Amen.

Discussion Questions

1. Have you ever thought of yourself as a light showing other people where to walk? What kind of light are you? A flashlight? Stoplight? Airport runway light?
2. Do your actions in the world reflect your beliefs? Can others see what you believe by how your light shines?

Thought for the Day:

God can put a light in your eyes and a glow on your face that will shine for others.

DAY 13

LIFE IS CHOICES, NOT CHANCES

by LYLE SANKEY (NATIONAL CHAMPION BULL RIDER)

"If God is for us, who can be against us?" (Romans 8:31).

Trying to stay on a two-thousand-pound Brahma bull that hates to have folks sitting on his back puts a lot of pressure on a cowboy! But sometimes people can put more pressure on you than a crazy bull.

In my rodeo career I've felt the push-and-pull competitive pressure in different forms. The most common was people's expectations and demands to conform. Trying to live up to what I believed others expected of me kept me from reaching my potential. Even when others did not try to apply outside pressure, for whatever reason, it soon became obvious that they were not the ones I could count on for support when things were toughest. Those who were there for the good times only seemed to disappear when I needed them the most. Over the years I've found that the ones who gave the most to me, without conditional returns expected, proved to be the real friends. They cared about me regardless of my performance in the arena and allowed me to be myself — sometimes less than the best, but free to learn and get better.

Life outside the arena is much the same. Group acceptance is all too often based on performance. "If I do what others expect, then I'll be part of the 'in' crowd. If I don't, I just may not fit in at all." Like those fair-weather friends in rodeo, "the in crowd" never seemed to be there when things got tough in everyday life.

Everyone loves a winner! When you are on top — in the limelight, popular, and so on — there's always a crowd close by. Conforming or giving in to pressure of what they expect from you will never help you reach your potential. In fact, it keeps you from becoming the person God intended you to to be.

As I realized that God accepts me and cares about me just as I am, I also understood that while I can't escape from all the crowd's efforts to intimidate and make me conform to their standards, I can keep the winning perspective that comes with knowing Jesus Christ. Romans 8:31 gives me a positive assurance of God's unconditional love: "If God is for us, who can be against us?"

Life is choices, not chances. I'm excited to know that because of God's love, I really do have a choice. Sometimes it helps just to reflect on that when the outside pressures get a little too great!

Prayer for the Day:

My Father, Thank You for accepting me and loving me just as I am. Help me to have the courage to stand against the negative pressures that try to take me from your love. Amen.

Discussion Questions:

1. How will peer pressure affect you today?
2. Why do we sometimes lower our standards to conform to the expectations of others?
3. How will Romans 8:31 help you to stand up for what you know is right?

Thought for the Day:

Jesus gives you inside braces to hold out against outside pressures.

Day 14

PLEASE PASS THE SALT

by Ben Nearn

"You are the salt of the earth, but if the salt has lost its savor, with what shall it be salted? It is thereafter good for nothing, but to be cast out, and to be trodden under foot of men" (Matthew 5:13).

Salt is used to spice up a bland meal. In biblical times there were no refrigerators or freezers, so to keep meat and other foods from spoiling, people used salt as a preservative. Jesus said that, as Christians, we have to be like salt to the earth.

The Christian life is not boring, but zestful! We make the world satisfying to God's palate. More importantly, we are preservatives of God's Word. We have to be stewards of this gift God has given us. We must learn God's Word, apply it, and live it.

We are also preservatives of the world; we keep it from spoiling. The salt shaker resembles God. We are in God as the salt is in the shaker. God, like the salt shaker, puts us in circumstances where a preservative is needed.

Prayer for the Day:

Dear Lord, You are almighty and all powerful. You can move mountains. I pray that Your abundant power will lift me up and help me to be salt to the earth. I pray that You will work through me and that it will be evident in my life that You live in me. Thank You for the fulfillment of Your promises. Amen.

Discussion Questions:

1. Who has been "salt" in your life? How?
2. Where is "salt" most needed in your school, sport events, hang-outs, etc.?
3. How can you be "salt" in these places?

Thought for the Day:

You are the salt of the earth. Has your salt lost its savor?

❑

Day 15

RUNNING FOR THE GRAND PRIZE

by Pat Byerly

"Do you not know that in a race all the runners run, but only one gets the grand prize? Run in such a way as to get the prize. Everyone who competes in the games goes into strict training. They do it to get a crown that will not last, but we do it to get a crown that will last forever. Therefore, I do not run like a man running aimlessly; I do not fight like a man beating the air. No, I beat my body and make it my slave so that after I have preached to others I myself will not be disqualified for the prize" (1 Corinthians 9:24-27).

"But those who hope in the Lord will renew their strength. They will soar on wings like eagles; they will run and not grow weary, they will walk and not be faint" (Isaiah 40:31).

As Christians, we run the ultimate race for eternal life. We are always training for the grand prize. When I'm running several miles I have to have water to drink. I also start praying to God to get me through the workout for the day. Life and the race are the same. The water gives me the strength and endurance. In the great race, the water is Jesus Christ. He gives the strength.

Life is one big race. Everyone participates in that race. Are you leading the pack, or are you back with everyone else? If we run without direction we will not win the grand prize. If our hope is in God, He will give us the endurance to finish the race.

Prayer for the Day:

Dear Lord, give me endurance to run for the grand prize. The crown You give will last forever. Give me Your strength to finish the race. Amen.

Discussion Questions:

1. Are you setting the pace, or are you back with the pack?
2. Are you running in the right direction?

Thought for the Day:

We can *let* things happen or we can *make* them happen.

❑

Day 16

CONSIDER OTHERS

by Shannon Albright

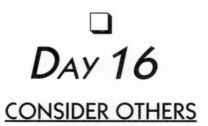

"Do nothing out of selfish ambition or vain conceit, but in humility consider others better than yourselves. Each of you should look not only to your own interests, but also to the interests of others" (Philippians 2:3-4).

Jesus Christ is a perfect example of considering others. In Philippians 2:6-8 we read how Jesus, "being in very nature God, did not consider equality with God something to be grasped, but made Himself nothing, taking the very nature of a servant, being made in human likeness. And being found in appearance as a man, He humbled Himself and became obedient to death — even death on a cross!"

We can graft this quality daily into our lives and become more Christlike. Being interested in other people can mean taking time to listen and showing your feelings, involving yourself in others' concerns and needs. Ask questions about them; be curious about their lives.

This might sound like a lot of giving, a lot of setting aside your own interests — and to tell you the truth, it is! But it's worth it! As the saying goes: "What you give is what you get..."

Jesus gave everything (and still does) — and wants us to to learn to give also.

Prayer for the Day:

Lord, thank You so much for taking an interest in me, revealing Your love for me. I pray that today will be a turning point in my life when I begin showing love and interest in others. I know it won't be easy, but by Your example and help I can do it! Thank You, Father. Amen.

Discussion Questions:

1. What does it mean to consider others better than yourself?
2. What are some things we do in "vain conceit" or "selfish ambition"?
3. Can you think of a couple of ways we show other people that we are not interested in them? What happens when we show that?

4. Name some easy, fun ways you can show your family members and friends that you're interested in them today.

THOUGHT FOR THE DAY:

Let your actions show your love for Christ.

❑

DAY 17

FULLNESS OF JOY

by CHARLOTTE BARNES

"These things have I spoken to you, that My joy may be in you, and that your joy may be made full" (John 15:11).

"These things" — what things? What did Jesus tell His disciples that would cause them to have fullness of joy? In verse nine of John 15, He had told them to abide in His love. His love is unconditional. He had given them clear instructions about unconditional love, telling them to love their friends: "Greater love has no one than this than to lay down his life for his friends." The best way to lay down our lives is to give up our own way. Laying down your life is more than dying physically for someone else; it is dying to self.

His further instruction from this passage was to keep His commandment. In Matthew 22:34-39 Jesus explains the greatest of the commandments. He said that the great and foremost commandment is to love the Lord with all your heart, all your soul, and all your mind. The second is to love your neighbor as yourself.

Is it possible to love God with all our heart, and not love our neighbor? Can we say we have fellowship with God and yet be critical of fellow Christians? If we withdraw from the fellowship of believers, we withdraw from fellowship with God. We can deceive ourselves into believing that our relationship with God is great, but if we have bitterness in our heart toward anyone, then our relationship with God is not valid.

We are also commanded in Scripture to love our family. Ephesians 6 gives clear instructions on family relationships. Children are instructed to honor their parents and parents are instructed to bring their children up in the discipline and instruction of the Lord.

Remember the promise Jesus made: If we will abide in his love and keep His commandments, we will experience fullness of joy.

Prayer for the Day:

Father, thank You for instructing us so clearly on how to be joyful. Help us to abide in Your love and obey Your commandments so that others may see Christ in us. Amen.

Discussion Questions:

1. How important is joy?
2. In what way can you lay down your life for your friends?
3. How can we avoid being critical of others' weaknesses?

Thought for the Day:

God wants our lives to be full of joy. His joy is our strength.

❑

DAY 18

WHERE'S THE BEEF?

by CHARLIE MCMATH

"Anyone who lives on milk, being still an infant, is not acquainted with the teaching about righteousness. But solid food is for the mature, who by constant use have trained themselves to distinguish good from evil" (Hebrews 5:13-14).

We've all seen the television commercial with the little old lady yelling, "Where's the beef?" Well, in the Christian life, what exactly is "the beef"?

When a person repents of his sins and receives Jesus Christ into his life, he becomes a spiritual infant and can comprehend only the foundational principles of God's Word, which the writer of Hebrews compares to milk. If you want to go on to a "beefy" Christian life, you need to do more than just spend a few minutes a day with Jesus. You need to take special advantage of good opportunities for prayer — while driving your car, or while walking across your school campus or work place. Other things that bring "beef " into your life include memorizing Scripture, helping in the ministry at your church, or spending time with the elderly at a local retirement home. The key is: Walk with Jesus all day from the time you get up until the time you go to bed.

God wants us to understand the deeper things of His Word by learning right from wrong, and by practicing doing right. In other words, you won't be ready for the "beef" until you begin to feed on God's Word and put into practice what you learn.

PRAYER FOR THE DAY:

Dear God, thank You for loving me enough to send Your only Son just for me! Praise You, Jesus, for all You endured on earth for me. Help me, Lord, to walk with You every day, all day. You know I want to in my heart; please give me the strength to practice this in my life today. Amen.

Discussion Questions:

1. Does your life consist of milk or meat?
2. What are some other practical ways you can add "beef" to your life?
3. What are some things that prevent us from walking with God all day long?
4. What is the first thing you can do to begin "beefing up" your life?

Thought for the Day:

Where there is an open mind, there will always be a frontier. Where there is a will, there is a way.

❑

Day 19

ALL THINGS WORK TOGETHER FOR GOOD

by Julie Fay

"All things work together for good to those who love God and are called according to His purpose" (Romans 8:28).

When joyful things happen to us, it is easy to believe this verse. When sad things happen to us, it's a hard verse to believe — but it's just as true then, and it can even be a source of comfort.

When I started high school, my greatest desire was to be on the pom-pom squad. When I didn't make it, my heart was broken. My goal had been shattered, and I was convinced there was nothing else I wanted to do. Well, God knew there was a place where I would fit in perfectly, and I had never even considered it. By not being on the pom-pom squad, I had time to try out for field hockey. I made the team, and over the past four years I have grown to love the team and the sport. This past year I was selected to be co-captain, and to my surprise I was selected to the all-conference first team. My earlier disappointment resulted in a greater thrill than being on the pom-pom squad, and I thank God for His blessing.

Prayer for the Day:

Dear Lord, thank You for the wonderful promises in Your Word. Help me truly love You the way You want me to. I belong to You and want to please You in everything I do. Amen.

Discussion Questions:

1. Describe a personal disappointment.
2. Describe a personal success.
3. Can you see anything good that came out of the disappointment?
4. Can you see God's hand in your life?

Thought for the Day:

Prayer consists of both talking to as well as listening to God. Are you listening?

DAY 20

PASSING THE TIME AWAY

by PATRICK HURLEY

"The world and its desires pass away, but the man who does the will of God lives forever" (1 John 2:17).

"Let's get together sometime." "I'll call you later." "I wish I had time for that." "There just aren't enough hours in the day." We have all said these phrases at one time or another. There is simply too much to do to accomplish everything we'd like to.

I suppose managing our time is one of the most difficult tasks we face on a daily basis. There is always something we're doing and always something we need to do. I know for myself I have to take a step back and focus on how wisely I am spending the time God has given me. Looking back, I can remember situations in which I have failed by becoming wrapped up in one task, not realizing I am neglecting other things in my life that are more important.

What we do with our time ought to reflect the values we place on what God has provided in our lives. 1 John 2:17 offers us wisdom on what really matters in life when it says, "The world and all its desires pass away, but the man who does the will of God lives forever."

PRAYER FOR THE DAY:

Father, thank You for giving us so many opportunities to devote our time to. Help us realize that the greatest way we can use our time is to love You and serve those around us. Help us today to give our time to You. Amen.

Discussion Questions:

1. What should influence my decisions about how to use my time?
2. What things in my life do I give too much time to? Too little time to?
3. Reflecting on 1 John 2:17, how should I use my time?
4. What is one thing I can do with my time today that would please Jesus?

Thought for the Day:

The only two things that will last forever are God's Word and people.

❑

Day 21

TRUST VS. FEELINGS

by Par Tolles

"Trust in the Lord with all your heart and lean not on your own understanding; in all your ways acknowledge Him, and He will make your paths straight" (Proverbs 3:5-6).

"There is a way that seems right to a man, but in the end it leads to death" (Proverbs 16:25).

When I was a boy, my dad became an instrument-rated pilot. One day as we were flying across central California in a dense cloud layer, we flew almost the entire trip on instruments. My eyes were fixed, as were my dad's, to the instrument panel of the plane. At one point it felt like the plane was turning yet the panel indicated that we were still at level flight. At another time I noticed that the instrument panel indicated that we were turning but it felt like we were going straight. I asked my dad about this.

"That's why we must keep our eyes on the instrument panel and act according to what it tells us," he said. "We must not act according to our feelings because our feelings can deceive us." When the manufacturer designed the plane, he included the instrument panel to guide the pilot so that he would not have to fly "according to his own understanding."

God, our manufacturer, has designed you and me. Our instrument panel is His Holy Word, the Bible. If we let it guide us and not act according to our feelings, He will show us when to stay at "level flight" and when to turn. Only in this way can we be led safely to our destination.

Prayer for the Day:

Father, show me the areas of my life in which I am "leaning on my own understanding." I don't want to make choices and decisions based on my feelings, because they can be contrary to Your Word. Show me in Your Word the course You want me to follow. Amen.

Discussion Questions:

1. In what areas of your life do you have a tendency to let your feelings guide you?
2. What does the Bible say about the way you feel (understand) in these areas of your life?
3. What steps can you take to fly God's way in these areas?

Thought for the Day:

Even when it feels like your course is accurate, be sure to check God's Word. You might be way off!

❑

DAY 22

THE GREAT ROAD MAP

by LANCE VAUGHN

"Thy Word is a lamp unto my feet and a light unto my path" (Psalm 119:105).

Isn't it interesting that when you slack off on your daily communication with God, problems seem to pile up? When I found problems mounting, I went to an older friend for some advice. I had some pretty tough questions about what is right and wrong in the Christian walk, and how to stay on the narrow path that God said to follow, yet still reach my personal goals.

My friend gave me some of the best advice I've ever received. He gave it to me by asking a simple question that, I hope, will also help you. He said, "Wouldn't it be odd if two Texans, who had never been further north than Dallas, got into a car and decided to drive to Minnesota without a road map?"

Many of us do something similar to that every day. We try to live a good life without reading the map. God gave us the greatest destination ever: to be like Jesus Christ. He gave us the greatest road map ever written to get to that destination: the Bible. The Bible shows how we can make it day by day in our busy, crazy world. After my friend shared this with me, I realized I needed to get to work. I needed to ask God my questions and spend some quiet time with Him and His wonderful map!

PRAYER FOR THE DAY:

Lord, thank You for Your Word. Thank You for its accuracy and relevance to my life. Help me spend this year focused on

Your Word. May this be the year of the Bible in our home. Amen.

Discussion Questions:

1. What direction are you headed?
2. How can you find a proper compass bearing for your life?
3. Tell about a time you were headed in the wrong direction and God's Word brought you back on the right path.

Thought for the Day:

When you get into your life's car and wonder which way to go, check the road map.

❑

Day 23

THE UNCHANGING MASTER

by Tricia Greenwood

"Jesus Christ is the same yesterday, today, and forever" (Hebrews 13:8).

This verse is encouraging to us because of our own inability to do anything about yesterday or tomorrow. Jesus, however, can change things, because He is not only Lord of today, He's also Lord of yesterday and Lord of tomorrow.

Why is it so important that Jesus is Lord of yesterday? We've all had problems in the past; we did things we wish we hadn't. We have no way of correcting those mistakes. But

Christ can! Through Him, we can be forgiven for the mistakes we've made. He can go back and fix up what we messed up!

Because Jesus is the same tomorrow as He is today, we can anchor ourselves in His stability. Our days will be filled with hard decisions and questions. When I'm deciding which college I should go to, which guy is the right one, or what kind of job I should get, I need Jesus to be with me to give me consistency in making good and right choices.

If you have any past problems that are still hanging on, let Jesus go back and take care of them for you. And let Him have a part in your new plans. If you feel things are too hectic, or you feel all alone, or your school life or life with your parents seems to be getting hard — remember that Jesus is the same forever, and He can handle anything.

Prayer for the Day:

Dear God, please forgive us for the mistakes we made in the past, and help us to have a new outlook on life and on improving our relationship with You. I pray that my family will draw closer to You than ever before. Amen.

Discussion Questions:

1. Have you asked forgiveness today for wrongs you might have committed yesterday, last month, or last year?
2. Do you keep God's Word in mind when you're planning tomorrow?
3. What are your plans for today?

Thought for the Day:

When talking with God today, thank Him for the stable rock He provides for your future.

❑

DAY 24

WHATCHA THINKIN' ABOUT?

by Scott Nissen

"Rejoice in the Lord always; again I will say, rejoice! Let your forbearing spirit be known to all men. The Lord is near. Be anxious for nothing, but in everything by prayer and supplication and thanksgiving let your requests be made known to God. And the peace of God, which surpasses all comprehension, shall guard your hearts and your minds in Christ Jesus. Finally, brethren, whatever is true, whatever is honorable, whatever is right, whatever is pure, whatever is lovely, whatever is of good repute, if there is any excellence and if anything worthy of praise, let your mind dwell on these things" (Philippians 4:4-8).

God spoke to me through this Scripture passage and changed my life. I had been a Christian for many years and truly loved the Lord, but you never would have known it from watching me, or if you could have read my mind. I was afraid of missing out on all the fun my non-Christian friends seemed to be having, so I started doing a lot of things I never thought I would.

Although it looked like I was having a great time on the outside, I was hurting and lonely on the inside. When I turned to God and His Word, it became clear that most of the things I was involved in were not pleasing to Him because they led my mind away from His will.

In your relationships — family, dating, friends — check to see if your thoughts are in line with truth. Are they honorable, right, pure, lovely? If you are in doubt, test your thoughts according to Philippians 4:8. Memorize this verse so it's always with you. Some things that helped me change my thought life are Christian music, Christian books, Christian friends, studying the Bible, and taking walks to pray.

Prayer for the Day:

Dear God, purify my heart. Help me to have only pure thoughts. Please show me thoughts that aren't right — so that this home can be solid, and my life be a blessing to You. Amen.

Discussion Questions:

1. Why does God want us to keep our thoughts pure and right and honorable?
2. What kind of music do you listen to? Have you listened to Christian artists who play that kind of music?

Thought for the Day:

Ask God for pure, honorable, and lovely thoughts today.

❑

Day 25

LIFT SOMEBODY UP

by Joan Chowning

"Bear one another's burdens, and thus fulfill the law of Christ" (Galatians 6:2).

Matthew, our six-year-old, stood in the doorway of his father's office. He didn't look ill, but he didn't look quite right. My husband, Gary, placed the phone down, saw the fragile look on our son's face and motioned Matthew to him. He reached out, lifted Matthew onto his lap and asked how he was doing.

Matthew began crying, softly at first, but soon his little body was shaking so that it was difficult to understand what he was saying. It seemed that Matthew had been given the privilege of accompanying a classmate outside the school building to dust the erasers. In the process of dusting them on the sidewalk, the erasers were thrown into the street to get dusted! Matthew and his classmate lost the privilege of dusting the erasers for the rest of the year.

As Matthew continued to sob, Gary's arms tightly encircled his tiny body. Ignoring his own damp cheek and shirt collar, he spoke lovingly to that little hurting person.

Bearing burdens is both a wonderful privilege and a responsibility. This sharing of heavy loads acts like glue in bonding the family closer together.

Sometimes lifting another person means nothing more than listening. Encouraging words and physical closeness mean a lot too. Sometimes we need to pray with the person who is burdened, and to keep on praying for them.

Our heavenly Father, the supreme bearer of burdens, sent His Son to shoulder our load and to take away all our sins. He has also given us opportunities to lift the loads of one another.

Prayer for the Day:

Lord, show us the ones who are down and need a lift. As we see those special needs, please give us the wisdom and grace to give a lift where it is needed. Amen.

Discussion Questions:

1. Do I pray regularly for my family?
2. Do I share my own problems, hurts, and burdens with my family?
3. Do I allow my parents or my children to be less than perfect, and to share their problems and cares?

THOUGHT FOR THE DAY:

In loving one another, we see our Savior more clearly.

❑

DAY 26

PRAYER CHANGES THINGS

by SHERRI VALVERDE

"Jesus said to her, 'Did I not say to you, if you believe, you will see the glory of God?' " (John 11:40).

It was September 17, 1987. At the side of the highway, an ambulance was being loaded with a boy who had fallen from the bypass above. The boy had broken a hip, two arms, and several ribs; he had also severed his liver and cracked a kidney. His face was unrecognizable because it had been crushed in the fall. The boy was my brother, Bobby, thirteen years old.

While my mother and sister went to the hospital, I stayed behind doing what I felt would be his only hope. I started calling friends and asking them to pray for my brother. I asked them to call their friends. People all over our town were praying for Bobby. Twice that night, he almost died. But God filled him with His strength and Bobby made it through the crisis.

A week later Bobby underwent an operation to reconstruct his face. Once again, everyone rallied together and prayed. Bobby returned from surgery looking like himself again.

The doctors had expected Bobby to be in the hospital for months, but he was released in just three weeks. They thought he might have to relearn a lot of things, but the only thing he could not remember was the terrible day of the accident and his stay in intensive care. They believed he would need a walker, but he walked farther than they believed possible the very first day. Bobby returned to school in less than two months after the accident.

PRAYER FOR THE DAY:

We are grateful, Lord, for all the ways both large and small that demonstrate to us Your amazing love and care.

DISCUSSION QUESTIONS:

1. In what ways has God worked in your life to show you His glory?
2. What Bible verses have you memorized about prayer?
3. What is the most wonderful thing you know to be true about prayer?

THOUGHT FOR THE DAY:

God will show us His power and glory when we pray.

DAY 27

LIVING IN THE LIGHT

by WILLIA DENNIS

"In the beginning God created the heavens and the earth. Now the earth was formless and empty, darkness was over the surface of the deep, and the Spirit of God was hovering over the waters. And God said, 'Let there be light,' and there was light. God saw that the light was good, and He separated the light from the darkness" (Genesis 1:1-4).

On a particularly busy day in the office, I was absorbed in my computer when over the intercom I heard the sweet, amiable voice of Tracy: "Willi, line one is for you." I was immediately irritated. The task I was trying to accomplish required concentration and it seemed the deadlines were arriving too quickly.

I picked up the telephone. "Mom!" shouted an excited little boy, and a smile crept over me. He continued excitedly: "Listen to this..." Then he read several verses from the book of Genesis, his voice rising and falling in little cascades of vocal intensity. Cameron had begun a Bible study lesson when the Holy Spirit opened his little mind to receive a beautiful truth: God had created light before He created the sun!

As I took in every word coming over that telephone, I could not have been any closer to my sweet little son. After I hung up, I began to think about the last time I had been as excited about God as Cameron was. How long had it been? God helped me see the difference between the electricity of my son's experience and the dullness I had felt the night before as I went through the motions of reading my Bible. "Lord," I prayed, "please ignite my spirit once again!" With childlike yearning, I cried to my Savior, and He responded.

The Scriptures exhort us to come as little children to God, innocent and uninhibited, with no pretenses. When we focus on Jesus Christ, the source of all light, the exuberance will splash out all around!

Prayer for the Day:

Thank You, God, for lighting up our lives with Your love. May Your light draw each of us closer to You and closer to each other. Amen.

Discussion Questions:

1. The symbol of light can mean many things: truth, omnipotent power, purity. In what other ways is the word *light* used to illustrate many of God's teachings in the Bible?
2. Does your family have a common vision?
3. What special work is God asking your family to do?

Thought for the Day:

God is light for our lives — light that can both guide us and excite us!

❑

Day 28

THEY'RE ONLY WORDS

by Wendi Spruney

"Let not many of you become teachers, my brethren, knowing that as such we shall incur a stricter judgment. For we all stumble in many ways. If any one does not stumble in what he says, he is a perfect man, able to bridle the whole body as well. No, if we put the bits into the horses' mouths so that they may obey us we direct their entire body as well. Behold, the ships also, though they are so great and are driven by strong winds, are still directed by a very small rudder, wherever the inclination of the pilot desires. So also the tongue is a small part of the body, and yet it boasts of great things. Behold, how great a forest is set aflame by such a small fire" (James 3:1-5).

One Monday morning a friend came up to me and said, "Wendi, I didn't know you did that sort of stuff!"

"What stuff?" I asked. What had I done?

I had gone to a party that weekend. Although I hadn't had any beer, my friend told me that someone was spreading a rumor that I had gotten drunk. But who? And why? I was really confused.

I found out later that my best friend, who hadn't even been at the party, had started the rumor. I didn't understand how she could say something so untrue and so cruel. Not only did the rumor hurt me, it hurt our friendship.

Rumors are like being stabbed in the back. You're injured before you know what's happening. And while the knife might be pulled out later, it's going to leave a permanent scar. Though we try to forgive, sometimes friendships can never be the same.

Each of us has dealt with rumors. You might have started one, listened to one, repeated one, or been the subject of one. Passing a rumor on is just as bad as starting one. We have the ability to quiet our tongues, but often, we just don't extinguish those small flames.

Prayer for the Day:

Dear Lord, teach me to speak so that others may feel loved. Teach me to listen so that others might feel needed. Teach me to care so that others might see You in my life.

Discussion Questions:

1. Do you try to say things that build up other people, or do you find fault with them?
2. How do you respond to rumors? Do you refuse to listen? Do you pass them along?

Thought for the Day:

Use your tongue to praise the Lord and ask blessings upon the people you know.

DAY 29

GIVING GOD YOUR VERY BEST

by JIM BRAWNER

"You must present a male without defect from the cattle, sheep, or goats in order that it may be accepted on your behalf" (Leviticus 22:19).

Israelite farmers were commanded to give the best of their flocks and of their harvest as an offering to the Lord. With this picture in mind, I am faced with the temptation every day to make compromises and give my second best instead of my best. I have to ask myself, "Am I letting God control my life, or is my lifestyle manipulating and deceiving me into thinking I'm the one in control?"

When I consider the sacrifice God made for me when He sent His Son, the decisions are much clearer (notice that I didn't say "easier"). The Christian walk is like a well-defined pathway through the Ozark forest. We can sense all the beauty of the forest from our position on the path. But when we stray away from the path, the forest becomes scary as we lose our sense of direction.

PRAYER FOR THE DAY:

Father, You know I want to do what is best. I don't always turn to You for making decisions. I know that Your way is not always the easy way, but it is the right way. When tempted to compromise, help me remember that less than my best is not good enough. Thanks for sending Your best for me. Amen.

Discussion Questions:

1. What compromises have you made recently in giving less than your best?
2. How can we help each other make the right decisions?
3. Why does God ask us to give our very best?
4. What was He doing when He gave Jesus to die on the cross?

Thought for the Day:

What pathway have you chosen to follow? Are you giving God your best?

❑

Day 30

TAKE ME FISHING AGAIN

by Joe White

"There is a time for everything, and a season for every activity under heaven: a time to be born and a time to die..." (Ecclesiastes 3:1-2).

"Pardner" had never been old enough to feel like a grandmother, so she always insisted that we call her by this informal, buddy-buddy name. Even though she's in her mid-nineties, she is still a kid at heart. The past three years have been rough for this dear lady who has earned the admiration of thousands of Kanakuk families through the years. For the first time she was unable to plant and water the more than five thousand flowers at our camps that were her personal handiwork during the previous twenty years. (This is where she earned her nickname, "The Flower Lady.")

Not long ago she called my two boys and me over to her house so she could give them her fishing rods and fishing tackle box. I knew what she was saying: "My fishing days are over." I didn't want my boys to take her fishing gear. She grew up on a country lake with a fishing pole attached to her hand, and has always been a fisherman par excellence. No one can catch and fry fish like Pardner. To her, fishing is like breathing. It's her love!

She insisted that we accept her gift. It broke my heart to walk away from her lakefront home with her fishing gear. I wish I had spent lots more time with her in her boat while she was still able. Now that it's too late, I regret being so selfish with my time.

Today I took her for a two-hour drive through Ozark country roads. What a great time we had, laughing, talking, and reminiscing over her many memories of our family's roots. I wish I could have many more times like this.

Time with those you love is like a rope being pulled through your hands. The harder you grab onto to it the more it burns.

Kids — your Daddy will never be thirty-nine again. Your grandparents don't have forever. Hey, teenagers — don't be in such a hurry to go out and have "fun." The fun is hidden in your mom's and dad's heart and can be unlocked with kindness. Parents — that sixteen-year-old will be off to college in two short years. Your eight-year-old won't be eight years old for long. These days will fly over your head like Canadian geese swiftly flying southward for winter.

My heart felt like breaking this year when I put my youngest child, Cooper, on his first school bus ride to kindergarten. I knew that in two blinks of an eye, I would be waving him off for his senior year in high school.

Jesus spent almost every day for three solid years with His disciples. They followed Him and took in His teaching until their last breath. His impact on their lives was immeasurable.

Go fishing together, before it's too late! Grab every second you can to spend with the ones you love. The party isn't down at the country club. It's right in your own living room.

Prayer for the Day:

Dear Lord, help us discover each other. Give us the keys to unlock each other's hearts in this treasure chest You have given us called home. Help us forgive each other like You have forgiven us. Amen.

Discussion Questions:

1. Can you think of a great idea to do together this week that would draw our family closer together?
2. How can we as a family capture some wonderful times together on a regular basis?
3. How could each member of our family organize priorities so that the people we love would get more out of our time?

Thought for the Day:

You gain the most when you give your time to those you love best.